Working with Adults: Values into Practice

A Learning and Development Manual

Jackie Martin and Sue Thompson

Learning for Practice

RHP

Russell House Publishing

First published in 2009 by:
Russell House Publishing Ltd.
4 St George's House
Uplyme Road
Lyme Regis
Dorset
DT7 3LS

Tel: 01297 443948
Fax: 01297 442722
e-mail: help@russellhouse.co.uk

British Library Cataloguing-in-publication Data:
A catalogue record for this book is available from the British Library.

ISBN: 978-1-905541-39-3

Editing and layout: Learning Curve Publishing, Wrexham

Printed by: Ashford Press, Southampton

About Russell House Publishing

Russell House Publishing aims to publish innovative and valuable materials to help managers, practitioners, trainers, educators and students.

Our full catalogue covers: social policy, working with young people, helping children and families, care of older people, social care, combating social exclusion, revitalising communities and working with offenders.

Full details can be found at www.russellhouse.co.uk and we are pleased to send out information to you by post. Our contact details are on this page.

We are always keen to receive feedback on publications and new ideas for future projects.

Contents

Series Editor's Foreword

About the *Learning for Practice* series

Education and training are essential underpinnings of high-quality professional practice. This series of learning and development manuals is therefore intended to provide foundations for promoting learning across the helping professions. Each manual offers guidance for new and experienced trainers alike, for managers and supervisors interested in promoting learning within their team or area of responsibility and for college or university lecturers wanting to go beyond simply delivering lectures.

The series has grown out of the Russell House *Theory into Practice* series of books which has been so successful in providing clear, short introductions to particular areas of theory as they apply to practice. Some of the manuals in this series are based on the issues covered in one or more of the books in that series, while other manuals have no direct connection with the series – although they all share a commitment to making an understanding of theory and professional knowledge more broadly accessible for practitioners and managers in order to try and make sure that our practice is *informed* practice.

The authors contributing to the series have a wealth of experience and expertise in promoting learning. Each manual therefore offers important insights, ideas and guidance that should be of great benefit in delivering high-quality learning and development events.

Experienced trainers, tutors and managers used to acting as learning facilitators should find the materials presented and the guidance given relatively straightforward. People with relatively little experience of running learning events will find the materials and guidance helpful, but may need additional support to translate the ideas given into successful learning outcomes. Such support may involve the backing of a more experienced colleague or the use of books and manuals specifically about running successful learning events, or indeed a combination of the two. So, whether experienced or not, this manual should offer a firm foundation on which to build.

About this manual

This manual is based on three books published in the *Theory into Practice* series: *Safeguarding Adults* by Jackie Martin, *Age Discrimination* by Sue Thompson and *Community Care* by Neil Thompson and Sue Thompson. The books share an emphasis on making sure that our work with 'vulnerable' adults is premised on a set of clear values. As the manual's subtitle indicates: it is a matter of putting 'values into practice'.

The manual presents a range of exercises designed to promote learning. These can be used to raise awareness, to deepen knowledge, to develop skills and to explore values. The authors have a wealth of experience and expertise that has been put to good use in developing this resource. They offer structured exercises that will provide a solid foundation for stimulating discussion, debate and exploration – but, above all, learning –

about these important issues. This makes this manual quite an invaluable resource.

Anyone committed to promoting learning, whether trainer, tutor, manager or practice teacher, will find this manual of great benefit and use. It deserves to be widely used, as the insights it offers can make a very important contribution to promoting high-quality professional practice in the care of adults.

Neil Thompson, series editor

The series editor

Neil Thompson is a Director of Avenue Consulting Ltd, a company offering training and consultancy across the 'people professions' – that is, the helping professions plus management, supervision and leadership more broadly (www.avenueconsulting.co.uk). He has held full or honorary professorial positions at four UK universities and is now a sought-after trainer, consultant and conference speaker.

Neil has qualifications in social work; training and development; mediation and alternative dispute resolution; and management (MBA) as well as a first-class honours degree and a PhD. He is a Fellow of the Chartered Institute of Personnel and Development, the Higher Education Academy and the Royal Society of Arts, as well as a Life Fellow of the Institute of Welsh Affairs. In addition, he is a member of the International Work Group on Death, Dying and Bereavement.

Neil is a highly respected author, with over 100 publications to his name, including several bestselling books. He is the editor of the US-based international journal, *Illness, Crisis & Loss* and also edits the e-zine, *Well-being* (www.well-being.org.uk). He has been a speaker at conferences and seminars in the UK, Ireland, Spain, Italy, the Netherlands, the Czech Republic, Norway, Greece, India, Hong Kong, Canada, the United States and Australia. He is the series editor for the Russell House *Theory into Practice* series of books. His website is at www.neilthompson.info.

Prospective authors wishing to make a contribution to the *Learning for Practice* series should contact Neil via his company website, www.avenueconsulting.co.uk

The authors

Jackie Martin is a principal lecturer at De Montfort University, Leicester. She is the programme leader for postqualifying courses for social workers and also teaches on the degree in social work. She has extensive experience of working with adults as well as children and young people in residential settings in both the statutory and voluntary sectors. She has worked for Nottinghamshire Social Services Department as an adult placement scheme co-ordinator, a social worker and team manager in community learning disability teams and as a supervising social worker in a team providing short breaks for disabled children.

Sue Thompson is a Director of Avenue Consulting Ltd, a company offering training and consultancy around social and workplace well-being issues. She has experience as a nurse, social worker, mentor and educator and has written, or co-written, several books and articles, including: *From Where I'm Sitting* (Russell House Publishing, 2002); *Age Discrimination* (Russell House Publishing, 2005); *The Social Work Companion* (Palgrave Macmillan, 2008) and *The Critically Reflective Practitioner* (Palgrave Macmillan, 2008). She is currently involved in cross-cultural research into the significance of reciprocity in the care of dependent older people.

Photocopying permission for the use of the worksheets and case studies

1. Permission to photocopy the worksheets and case studies is only given to **individuals or organisations who have bought a copy of the manual** and then only for distribution at the local level within their organisation. The price of this manual has deliberately been kept affordable to smaller organisations. It is therefore expected that, as a matter of honour, larger organisations - for example, national or county-wide statutory or voluntary organisations - who might want to use the photocopiable material in numerous locations, will buy a copy of the manual for use in each locality where they are using the material.

2. If a **trainer or an educational organisation** wants to copy and distribute these handouts to assist their work with clients in organisations where they are training, it is expected that they will buy a copy of the book for each organisation where they undertake such training and - in line with the principles set out in point 1 (above) - a copy for each locality when they are training in a large organisation at multiple locations. This expectation is based on respect for the author's copyright and the view that providing manuals in this way will add to the benefits delivered in the training. The publisher and authors therefore seek trainers' active support in this matter.

3. Under no circumstances should anyone sell photocopied material from this manual without the express permission of the publisher.

If in doubt, anyone wanting to make photocopies should contact the publisher, via email at: help@russellhouse.co.uk.

Other photocopying permissions

Anyone wishing to copy all or part of the worksheets and case studies *in any context other than set out here* should first seek permission in the usual way:

- either via Russell House Publishing
- or via the Copyright Licensing Agency.

Anyone wishing to copy any other part of this manual in any context, beyond normal fair trading guidelines, should first seek permission in the usual way:

- either via Russell House Publishing
- or via the Copyright Licensing Agency.

Electronic supply of the worksheets and case studies

A PDF of the pages of this manual, on which the worksheets and case studies appear, is available free, by email from RHP, to purchasers of the book who complete and return the licence request at the end of the manual.

Please note that anyone who is reading this in a copy of the manual from which the tear-out coupon has been removed would need to buy a new copy of the manual in order to be able to apply for the electronic materials.

The following terms and conditions for use of the electronic materials apply in all cases:

Terms and conditions for use of the worksheets and case studies from *Working with Adults*

1. Buying a copy of *Working with Adults* and completing the form at the back of this manual gives the individual who signs the form permission to use the materials in the PDF that will be sent from RHP for their own use only.

2. The hard copies that they then print from the PDF are subject to the same permissions and restrictions that are set out in the 'photocopying permission' section at the front of this manual.

3. Under no circumstances should they forward or copy the electronic materials to anyone else.

4. If the person who signs this form wants a licence to be granted for wider use of the electronic materials within their organisation, network or client base, they must make a request directly to RHP fully detailing the proposed use. All requests will be reviewed on their own merits.

> • If the request is made when submitting this form to RHP, the request should be made in writing and should accompany this form.

> • If the request is made later, it should be made in an email sent to help@russelhouse.co.uk, and should not only fully detail the proposed use, but also give the details of the person whose name and contact details were on the original application form.

RHP and the authors expect this honour system to be followed respectfully, by individuals and organisations whom we in turn respect. RHP will act to protect authors' copyright if they become aware of it being infringed.

Introduction

This manual is designed to be a companion volume to three books in the 'Theory into Practice' series; *Community Care*, *Age Discrimination* and *Safeguarding Adults*. It provides training resources which offer food for thought in addressing some of the key issues facing those who support adults experiencing difficulties. In Part One we explore some general issues that relate to practice across a wide range of human services work. While we advocate that all work in this field should be underpinned by anti-discriminatory values, we have chosen in Part Two to focus more particularly on the need to challenge inequality and value diversity. This is to mirror the importance it is accorded in all books in the Theory into Practice series. Working with and supporting service users might seem to some to be fairly straightforward but it requires a great deal of sensitivity and an awareness of how service users can be discriminated against in a variety of ways and at a number of different levels. The exercises have therefore been written as aids to helping you as the trainer to promote practice that is underpinned by understanding. Where an exercise requires the use of worksheets, these can be found directly after the exercise. Case studies can be found at the end of the manual.

The timings suggested for each exercise are approximate as it very much depends on the numbers of participants you are training and the individual participants themselves. If you choose to use all of the exercises from one topic, they can be done in a different order to that suggested, although some exercises do build on work done in earlier ones. You can use exercises on a stand-alone basis and you could mix and match from different sections if this suits your needs. In some sections we have suggested introductory exercises as 'ice breakers'. These are linked wherever possible to the theme of the session so serve as a way into the subject as well as a lighthearted start to your session and a way to get to know your group.

If you are new to training you might want to consult introductory books on the subject such as Jolles (2005) or Klatt (1999) which is a comprehensive volume, details of which can also be found in the further reading section. What follows can work as a checklist for beginners but, if you are an experienced trainer, then you can safely skip what follows and move onto Part One.

Things to think about in planning for a session

Having the right exercises and activities for a session is important, but is only a part of your planning. For a successful session you should also address the following:

- You will also need to prepare your resources. These might be flip chart paper and pens, enough photocopies of any exercises for the whole group, spare A4 paper and pens, sticky labels for participants to write their names on or whatever else is required in the session.

- If you are using any electrical equipment such as a laptop with a data projector, make sure this is working and you have time to set it up before the session starts.

• You need to think of the layout of the room. The books in the suggested further reading go into great detail about different styles of room layout. You need to think about whether you want participants to have access to tables to write on or whether you want a less formal style without tables. Do you want a very formal layout with rows of participants or a more informal style (which lends itself better to this type of training) and have participants in a circle or horseshoe shape? Arriving early and having things set out ready gives a good message to participants when they arrive.

• Preparing a programme makes it clear to participants what they are doing throughout the day and when breaks will take place. It can be useful to remind people about the length of such breaks and to give a clear message about the time they are expected to return. The length of break will depend on a number of factors, but it needs to be borne in mind that it may take some time for a large group to get refreshments if these are provided. If you are going to provide refreshments then they will, of course, need to be organised in advance. If participants are required to organise their own then they will need to be aware of this in advance.

• Preparing a register for participants to sign will give you a record of attendance and may be required for fire regulation or health and safety reasons.

• It can be useful to have produced for yourself a set of notes to serve as prompts, especially if you do not plan to follow the exercises in the sequences offered, or you want to adapt or add other exercises.   .

Things to remember during the session

• Introduce yourself and state the purpose of the session.

• Go through any 'housekeeping' announcements, such as fire procedures, where toilets are, etc.

• Ask participants to introduce themselves.

• Trainers often start by agreeing a list of 'rules' for the day. This can be done by asking participants what they think is important, then adding anything they miss that you feel is important, remembering to stress confidentiality. Other suggestions might include 'to respect individuals', 'to listen to each other', 'to come back from breaks on time' and so on.

• Give clear instructions about each exercise. It is often enough to do so verbally, but more complex instructions may need to be spelt out in a handout or on a flip chart or board.

• When small groups are discussing the activity you have set them, allow them to start the discussion but then go and listen to each group to make sure they have understood the task and are focused on it as well as being there to make suggestions or answer any questions.

• The timings that are suggested are approximate. Be prepared to be flexible and allow extra time if needed or move on to another exercise if it is clear that enough time has been spent on it. Timings are difficult to gauge, as an activity can work really well with one group and they can quite happily work on it for a long time whereas another group may finish it really quickly.

• When you are taking feedback from the small groups or pairs, you need to acknowledge what has been said and comment on what is useful or interesting about it. Try and make links between what has been said throughout the session by participants and the work that you are doing with the group. This shows that you value the contributions being made and helps participants to make links themselves.

What to do at the end of the session

It is useful to obtain feedback from participants at the end of a day so that you can evaluate the usefulness of the exercises and the quality of your performance. You can devise a form for this or you can ask people to give verbal feedback or write their comments on a piece of flipchart as they leave. You need to think about what you want to find out from participants to help you plan future sessions. You will probably want to know how helpful the session was - what worked well and what was unhelpful. You may also want to have feedback on the venue and facilities or to ask about future learning needs.

What to do after the session

It is useful to analyse the feedback and reflect on how the session went. If you deliver the session with someone else, it can be helpful to meet to discuss how the session went and to agree any improvements for future training events.

A note about timing

You will notice that there is a suggested timeframe for each exercise. This has been added as an approximate guide for leading the exercise, and to help with the overall planning for the event. The timings, however, are only approximations, and it is up to the leader to decide how best to pace each exercise for the benefit of the participants.

A note on the three books

It is not necessary for you to have read the three books the manual is based on before using the exercises in the manual, but we would recommend that you do so, as the books will give you a solid foundation of knowledge and understanding to inform your learning and development work.

Training Exercises: General

Part One comprises a set of exercises which reflect some of the key themes and issues featured in the three books with which this manual is linked. The choice of which particular aspects to focus on is, ultimately, a personal one informed by our experience and the personal and professional values we hold, but we feel that what follows is a reflection of what needs to be explored and debated if the disadvantage and disempowerment experienced by vulnerable and disenfranchised adults is to be challenged and well-informed and critically reflective practice in the human services promoted. We would therefore expect anti-discriminatory practice and the knowledge and values bases that underpin it to feature not only in Part Two, where there is a more specific focus on discrimination and oppression, but also in the discussions that the exercises in this section produce. In providing a separate set of exercises in Part Two it is not our intention to suggest that these issues can be seen in isolation from other aspects of people's lives and the work we undertake with them, but rather to say that they are so important that they deserve extra attention.

Promoting Dignity

Setting the Scene

Promoting dignity is an important value which should underpin the provision of care and support to vulnerable adults, because to deny a person their dignity is to deny him or her their status as a human being worthy of respect. It relates not only to hands-on care, but also to the provision of care and support in a much wider sense, including care management, advocacy, housing provision and so on.

The issue of dignity in care is at the heart of a recent government initiative - the Dignity in Care initiative - policy guidance which followed consultation with a wide range of people involved in social care provision, about what people want, and should expect, from service providers. The ten different aspects of dignity which comprise the 'Dignity Challenge' are described in the following quotation from the guidance produced by the Social Care Institute for Excellence (2006):

> The Dignity Challenge: High quality care services that respect people's dignity should:
>
> - have a zero tolerance of all forms of abuse
> - support people with the same respect you would want for yourself or a member of your family
> - treat each person as an individual by offering a personalised service
> - enable people to maintain the maximum possible level of independence, choice and control
> - listen and support people to express their needs and wants
> - respect people's right to privacy
> - ensure people feel able to complain without fear of retribution
> - engage with family members and carers as care partners
> - assist people to maintain confidence and a positive self-esteem
> - act to alleviate people's loneliness and isolation. [p.7]

While it focuses specifically on dignity in eldercare, the issues that this initiative highlights are, we think you'll agree, relevant to all individuals who find themselves in situations where they have to rely on others. We would urge you to keep the Dignity Challenge in mind when using the exercises that follow and consider whether the discussions that ensue provide a challenge to, or reinforce, this particular overview of what constitutes caring with dignity.

In attempting to challenge the conceptualisation of adults who receive care and support as 'different from' or 'lesser than' other adults, the promoting of both dignity and an ethos of working in partnership can be said to be mutually supportive. As such, most of the content of the three *Theory into Practice* books should provide useful background material but, more particularly, we would highlight the following discussion topics:

Community Care: quality of life, spirituality, balancing rights and risk, challenging stereotypes

Safeguarding Adults: social model of vulnerability, abuse and the standards and values associated with them

Age Discrimination: infantilisation; dehumanisation; multiple oppression

Promoting Dignity - What Does it Mean?

Aim

When dignity is referred to in reports and policy initiatives, there is often an assumption that it is a well-understood term. We would argue that this is not necessarily the case and that definitions such as this involve value judgements about what does and does not compromise an individual's dignity. Given the links between dignity and such important issues as human rights, well-being and self-esteem, it is important to take time out to explore it rather than make assumptions about it.

Materials

Copies of the worksheet - 'Promoting Dignity - What Does it Mean?; flip chart paper and pens; Blutack or equivalent; white board or flip chart for recording feedback.

Timing

This can be flexible but we would suggest that you allow between about an hour and 80 minutes.

Notes for trainer

This worksheet invites discussion about a potentially broad-ranging topic and so you may need to encourage participants to focus on their specific task. As there is the potential for a lot of time to be spent on choosing a scenario, it can be useful to have some examples which can be drawn on if participants are having trouble identifying or deciding on one.

Activity

  • This is a group discussion exercise. It is designed to get the participants 'unpicking' this taken-for-granted term and exploring whether dignity has a universal meaning.

  • Divide the main group into four subgroups or sets of partners. Explain what the exercise is about and then distribute the accompanying worksheet and a pen and sheet of flip chart paper to each group, asking that someone records the key points that arise from their discussion. Allocate each group one of the aspects of dignity identified on the worksheet. (Allow 5 to 10 minutes for this phase.)

  • Once the groups have had a reasonable amount of time for discussion (approximately 30 minutes) ask them to display their completed flip chart sheets on a wall, if allowed, or place on a table so that each group's contribution can be read by the others (10 minutes or so).

• Reconvene the main group and use what the small group discussions produced as the basis for a plenary discussion about whether dignity is perceived in the same way by all and, if not, the implications of this for policy and practice (15 to 20 minutes).

• Use the last 5 minutes of the session to sum up the main themes that have emerged.

Promoting Dignity - What Does it Mean?

According to the Social Care Institute for Excellence (SCIE, 2006), research with older people, their carers and care workers has identified dignity with four overlapping ideas:

- Respect
- Privacy
- Self-esteem, self-worth and a sense of oneself
- Autonomy

In terms of the one aspect your group has been allocated, identify a situation in which someone in the group feels that the dignity of a vulnerable adult (not necessarily an older adult) was compromised in this way. Consider the following questions;

    1. Does everyone in your group agree that this was an issue about dignity?

    2. Did the person in question present it in those terms?

    3. Do you think that other people involved in the scenario saw it as a loss of dignity?

    4. Do you think that dignity can be compromised in ways other than the ideas highlighted in the above list?

Promoting Dignity - What Can We Do About it?

Aim

The purpose of this exercise is to build on the earlier discussions around how dignity can be defined and encourage participants to think more about what needs to be challenged and how they might do so.

Materials

White board or flip chart for recording feedback; additional flip chart sheets and pens; copies of Case Studies 1 to 4 and accompanying questions.

Notes for trainer

The suggested timings are given on the assumption that each group will look at a different case study, so that there will be four sets of feedback. If time or numbers do not allow for this, then it could be adapted so that each group looks at the same case study you have chosen for the purpose. Both options are likely to generate useful material for discussion. You may need to give time prompts to remind people that they need to attend to all of the questions.

Timing

It is difficult to be precise, but you will probably need to allocate between an hour and a half and two hours for this exercise.

Activity

• This is a group activity which works well with pairs or small groups using case studies to generate discussion, but could also be used by individuals.

• Split the main group into four smaller groups or pairs. Explain the purpose of the exercise and hand out to each of the four groups a different case study from those numbered 1 to 4 at the end of the manual (allow 5 to 10 minutes). Then ask them to read through the study and work through the questions in turn. When they have done so (allow about 30 minutes or so), reconvene the main group and invite a spokesperson from each group to briefly explain the context they were exploring and the main points that arose from their discussions. About 10 to 15 minutes should be sufficient for each group's presentation and, during this process, you will need to make a brief record on a flip chart or board of the key issues that arise from each. Once all the feedback has been given, you should be left with a record that provides the basis, in the final 10 to 15 minutes or so, for pulling out themes, concerns, tips, strategies and so on.

Promoting Dignity, Promoting Change

Aim

Promoting dignity often involves promoting change, and so it is important when working with adults to think about power issues. For example, we need to think about who has the power to promote change. Are some people or organisations more powerful than others? Who has the power to define what dignity means? This activity is designed to focus more on how to promote change than on what needs changing.

Materials

Copies of the worksheet - Promoting Dignity, Promoting Change; notepaper or a sheet of flip chart paper and pen for each group; white board or flip chart for displaying questions and recording feedback.

Timing

Allow about an hour for this exercise.

Notes for trainer

The exercise can be used in situations where all participants are from the same organisation. However, if you have a number of organisations represented, the resulting discussions are likely to be more broad ranging, especially if people from the same organisation are encouraged to join different groups and share their perspectives with those from other organisations. Participants may need to be reminded that change can take place at a number of different levels, making it important to think about where constructive criticism needs to be targeted if change is to be promoted.

It needs to be borne in mind that this exercise requires a degree of conceptual thinking, and so you will need to use your judgement to gauge whether it will work for your particular group.

Activity

• While this group activity is broadly about promoting dignity, it focuses more specifically on promoting change where it is felt that dignity has been compromised. It involves participants working in small groups to explore what avenues or strategies are open to them for achieving change.

• After explaining the purpose of this exercise, ask each group to spend 20 to 30 minutes considering the questions on the accompanying worksheet before meeting up again in the main group to share the thoughts that have arisen from within the small groups. Leaving about 15 to 20 minutes for this phase should allow enough time to draw out the key points from what emerges.

Promoting Dignity, Promoting Change

1. Within your organisation is the promotion of dignity a policy issue or is it down to individuals to work on as they see fit?

2. In what ways can you promote change in your organisation?

3. Are there barriers to change within your organisation? If so, what can you do about them?

Promoting Dignity - is it Working?

Aim

This is a useful exercise for drawing out the implications of earlier discussions for practice. It is about evaluating whether attempts to promote dignity are working for everyone concerned: that is, part of a value base, and not just a tokenistic approach which 'ticks the right boxes' or a case of following guidelines without really understanding their significance. Being called on to evaluate dignity will help to reinforce the earlier discussions about what constitutes dignity.

Materials

Copies of the worksheet - Dignity Audit Guidelines; extra flip chart sheet and pen for each group; white board or flip chart for recording feedback.

Timing

Allow between an hour and 90 minutes for this exercise.

Notes for trainer

While this is presented as an exercise in two stages, each part could stand alone. As participants are asked to consider what they themselves would expect in terms of preserving dignity, they may talk about situations that they or those close to them have experienced and which may have been distressing. Vigilance and sensitivity are therefore called for to ensure that participants feel comfortable with what they are being asked to do.

Activity

> • This is designed to be used as group activity but, as it in worksheet format, it could also be carried out by individuals as an aid to learning.

> • Once the point of this part of the exercise has been explained, the main group needs to be split up into four pairs or small groups, allocating each a number between one and four. Explain to the groups that they will each be focusing on a particular service user group, even though this might not match with the field of work in which they are actually involved (5 to 10 minutes).

> • Then, allocate each group a context as follows:

>> - Group 1 - a residential establishment for adults who have a severe learning disability.
>> - Group 2 - a nursing home for older people.
>> - Group 3 - a hostel for homeless people with mental health problems

- Group 4 - a daycentre for adults with pre-senile dementia.

• Step 1 - Ask the participants to imagine they are users of the service their group has been allocated and think about what they would expect in terms of being treated with dignity. If the discussion does not start spontaneously, it can be useful to give participants a few minutes to think this through on their own, then to share thoughts with a partner, then for each set of partners to double up and share thoughts with another set of partners. This technique usually works well to stimulate discussion, but whether it is workable will depend to a certain extent on the size of the group (20 to 30 minutes).

• Arrange a short break between stages one and two to allow participants to come out of the role they have been asked to assume and return to their own perspective and the training situation.

• Step 2 - Now ask the participants to imagine that they are inspectors visiting the establishment they have been allocated to check whether the service provided is living up to its promise to 'promote the dignity of individuals at all times'. When you are sure that they understand the task, give each person a copy of the Dignity Audit Guidelines worksheet and allow them time to work through the questions (about 20 minutes should be sufficient).

• When the groups have had sufficient time to consider all of the questions on the worksheet, reconvene as a main group and, considering each question on the worksheet in turn, ask for feedback from each of the four groups (20 minutes or so). Keep a brief running record of the contributions made so that you can spend the last few minutes drawing out the key issues that have arisen, paying particular attention to anything that links the different perspectives covered in steps 1 and 2.

Dignity Audit Guidelines

1. What might you hear (or not hear) that would provide evidence?

2. What could you read that might provide evidence? For example, which documents might give you a clue to an organisation's values or practices?

3. What else might you see or be looking for on your visit that might provide positive or negative evidence?

4. Who would you want to talk to during your visit?

Suggested Further Reading

Brown, C. (ed.) (2006) *Vulnerable Adults and Community Care: A Reader*, Exeter, Learning Matters.

Bytheway, B., Bacigalupo, V., Bornat, J., Johnson, J. and Spurr, S. (eds) (2002) *Understanding Care, Welfare and Community: A Reader*, London, Routledge.

Commission for Social Care Inspection (2006) *Making Choices: Taking Risk - A Discussion Paper*, London, CSCI.

Jolles, R. (2005) *How to Run Seminars and Workshops: Presentation Skills for Consultants, Trainers and Teachers*, New Jersey, NJ, John Wiley and Sons

Klatt, B. (1999) *The Ultimate Training Workshop Handbook*, Maidenhead, McGraw-Hill.

Lustbader, W. (1991) *Counting on Kindness: The Dilemmas of Dependency*, New York, The Free Press.

Malone, C., Forbat, L., Robb, M. and Seden, J. (eds) (2005) *Relating Experience: Stories from Health and Social Care*, London, Routledge.

Moss. B. (2005) *Religion and Spirituality*, Lyme Regis, Russell House Publishing.

Pritchard, J. (2007) *Working with Adult Abuse: A Training Manual for People Working with Vulnerable Adults*, London, Jessica Kingsley Publishers.

Social Care Institute for Excellence (2006) *Adult Services Practice Guide 09: Dignity in Care*, London, SCIE.

Thompson, N. and Thompson, S. (2007) *Understanding Social Care*, 2nd edn, Lyme Regis, Russell House Publishing.

Working in Partnership with Service Users and Carers

Setting the scene

The concept of 'partnership' is considered in *Community Care*. Chapters 3 and 8 consider 'making partnership work.' Chapter 4 of *Safeguarding Adults* discusses 'issues in relation to family carers' and Chapter 5 explores service user involvement and participation. Partnership working with service users and carers is increasingly being seen as important by practitioners and legislators. It is an essential element of practice, but one which can be difficult to truly incorporate in practice. It is easy to pay 'lip service' to this concept, and so the exercises are designed to challenge practice which does this and to encourage good practice.

The definition of 'partnership' is crucial to this session, and for that reason the session starts with a consideration of it. Sometimes people can get 'stuck' in their practice and the patterns that are formed in the way that service users are worked with is one such pattern. If someone's concept of partnership working is about making decisions on other people's behalf, which they believe to be in their best interest, and then persuading the person they are supporting that it is the best option for them, then they need to reconsider the concept. A better understanding of the concept of 'partnership', as well as the complexity of working in partnership with service users and carers, is essential if good practice is to be developed.

Introductory Exercise

Aim

This exercise is designed to get participants to draw on their experience of life in general to begin to explore the potential benefits of working together.

Materials

Pen and paper for participants may be useful.

Timing

About 15 minutes.

Notes for trainer

Whether or not you want to use this or any introductory exercise will depend on your group but it is included so that you can make your own decision. Its purpose is to provide a light introduction to the day and to get everyone to contribute right at the very beginning of the session.

If the group consists of people who don't already know each other, you could incorporate this with introductions, whereas if you are working with an established team of people, you won't need to do so, unless you need them to introduce themselves to you.

Activity

• This is an exercise for individuals and pairs.

• Ask each participant to think of a partnership which doesn't already exist but which they think will work well – for example, two comedians, politicians, athletes, cartoon characters or fictional characters and to share their idea with the group.

• Ask participants to think of why these partnerships might work.

• Allow a couple of minutes for thinking time and then ask the participants to dicuss the ideas with the person they are sitting next to. Allow a further 5 minutes for discussing in pairs.

Exercise 2.1.

Lessons from What Works Well

Aim

This exercise is based on the principles of Appreciative Inquiry (Cooperrider, Whitney and Stavros, 2003), which is where principles are drawn from a consideration of something that is good or works well.

Materials

Copies of the worksheet - Working in Partnership with Service Users and Carers; flip chart paper and pens for each group; white board or flip chart for recording feedback.

Timing

Allow about an hour for this exercise.

Activity

- Individual and small group work using a worksheet to promote discussion.

- Ask participants to consider question 1 on the worksheet individually and, once they have done that, to also complete question 2 on their own. The idea behind this is to encourage them to identify principles behind partnership working from a partnership they are familiar with. Allow about 15 minutes for this part of the exercise.

- After they have answered questions 1 and 2 on their own, ask participants to form groups of about 4 or 5 people (depending on the size of your main group).

- Ask each group to answer question 3 and record their list on flip chart paper. Each group will be making a list of what they think makes a good partnership using the examples each member has thought of for questions 1 and 2. Allow about 15 to 20 minutes for the groups forming and the subsequent discussion.

- Ask each group to share their list with the other groups and note any striking themes or differences.

Working in Partnership with Service Users and Carers

1. Working on your own, think of a situation where you have either been part of or have seen a successful partnership. This partnership might be a personal relationship, a working or business relationship or even taken from a sport context.

2. When you have thought of an example of successful partnership working, write a list of what was it about the people, the context and the relationship within the partnership that made it successful.

3. In a small group, share your examples and the lists of what made them good examples of partnership. Now agree a list of 'what makes a good partnership' and record your group's list.

Partnership Case Study

Aim

The idea of the exercise is to encourage participants to apply the model of good partnership they have devised themselves and apply it to a situation of working with service users.

Materials

Copies of Case Study 5.1.; flip chart paper and pen for each group; white board or flip chart for recording feedback.

Timing

Allow about an hour and a half for this exercise.

Activity

- Small group work.

- Ask the same groups to consider Case Study 5.1 and answer the questions at the end of the study. The questions are designed to encourage the participants to think about what partnership means when applied to working with carers and service users. Question 1 asks 'What issues does this situation highlight and what dilemmas does it pose for those being called in to intervene?' When going and talking to each group as they answer this question, encourage them to think about ageist assumptions. *Age Discrimination* provides you with a helpful reminder of the issues of ageism in preparation for this session. Allow about 30 minutes for discussion.

- Ask each group to feed back what they have discussed in relation to this question before they embark on the following questions. When taking feedback from each group ensure that consideration is given to:

> - not making assumptions and the need for further information to be obtained.
> - obtaining information from Cyril himself.
> - Cyril's needs.
> - Cyril's wishes.
> - Ann's views and her ability to continue to support Cyril.

• When the issues in relation to working with Cyril have been discussed in the main group, ask each small group to discuss questions 2 and 3. These two questions ask the group to look at the list they made of 'what makes a good partnership' and discuss how this can be applied to working firstly with Ann and then with Cyril. When each group is discussing these questions it would be helpful to go round and ensure they are 'on track' as regards the aim of the exercise (see overleaf). Encourage participants to propose practical ways of working with Cyril and Ann in a positive way - for example gathering their views of the situation and listening to both of them, including both in decisions and any meetings held about Cyril. Allow about 30 minutes for group discussion.

• Finish this part of the session by asking groups to feed back to the whole group and sum up the positive suggestions for working with both Ann and Cyril in a way which is consistent with the positive views of partnership working from the beginning of the session.

Creative Lessons

Aim

This is designed to help participants to explore the concept of partnership from the perspective of someone using, rather than providing, a service.

Materials

A piece of flip chart paper and a collection of coloured pencils, crayons, markers for each group; Blutack or equivalent/sticky tape (if allowed to put posters on wall).

Timing

Allow about an hour for this exercise.

Activity

• This exercise is designed to provide an energiser if it is done after a lunch break, but also to appeal to the creative side of your participants.

• It is continuing thinking about partnership, but expressed in a different way from the rest of the day. Divide your main group into smaller groups - this can be the same as in the morning session or different groupings to ensure people have the opportunity to work with different people. Provide each group with flip chart paper and a range of coloured pencils, crayons or markers. Ask them to imagine they are a group of service users and carers and to design a poster entitled 'partnership - what it means to us'. Explain that the poster is to depict visually how carers and service users would want to be worked with by human services workers.

• Allow plenty of time for the groups to prepare for this activity before they start to design the poster and prompt them to think through what they want to depict before they start working on the posters. Allow about 30 minutes for the discussion and activity but more if you see that the groups need extra time to complete this task.

• When the posters are finished, display them in a 'picture gallery' and ask each group to explain the thinking behind their poster.

• This activity should require little summing up by you, but you may feel you need to draw attention to the main themes that have emerged in the posters.

Exercise 2.4.

Values into Action

Aim

The aim here is to stimulate further thought and discussion about working together, especially in situations where there are obstacles to putting the value into action.

Materials

Copies of Case Study 5.2; flip chart sheet and marker for each group, white board or flip chart for recording feedback.

Timing

Allow about an hour for this exercise.

Activity

• Small group work using worksheets.

• This is the last part of the session and for it you will return to Cyril and Ann. Ask each small group to read Case Study 5.2 and address the first two tasks on the worksheet.

• Take feedback from tasks one and two before groups start task three. The first two tasks are designed to be practical so that participants will start to apply what they have been considering about partnership working to their own practice. They are asked to first draw up an action plan on how to include Cyril in a review process and secondly how to work more effectively with Ann. Allow 20 minutes for each task to be addressed – in other words, 40 minutes in total.

• As part of your preparation for this exercise it would be helpful if you read *Safeguarding Adults,* Chapter 5. Participants will consider the difficulty of including Cyril now that his dementia is more advanced. It is important to point out to participants that the principle here is to include him as fully as possible. Points that are worth considering are whether Cyril wants to be part of a meeting about him or whether he would rather be included in a different way. If he wants to be included in the meeting, the timing might be important, as there may be times of the day which are better for Cyril than others. Other considerations may be using photographs with Cyril rather than written words if he is no longer able to understand them, including him in discussions about his care routine and having these views represented at the review. Importance should be placed on how Cyril is prepared for the review, how it is explained to him as well as where it takes place, as he may become disorientated. In other words, every aspect of the review process should be thought through to see how Cyril can be worked with in a spirit of partnership.

• The second task asks the group to consider how to work with Ann, and the groups should form an action plan for working with her. This plan might include asking Ann how she wants to be worked with and agreeing contact times and arrangements with her as well as including her in relevant meetings and decisions about her father as appropriate.

• Once the groups have discussed both tasks, ask them to feedback to the whole group their thoughts on both tasks. Ask for feedback on task one first from each group and then go on to task two. Use the notes above to bring out points from the discussion.

• The third task should take about 20 minutes and really forms the summing up of the day's session. The groups are asked to write a list of 'dos' and 'don'ts' for working in partnership with service users and carers and this should draw on all of the activities of the day. Ask each group to feedback their thoughts and obtain some agreement from the group on collating these lists as pointers for good practice. You will need to ask the group how they want the pointers to be used in their work setting(s).One idea is that the pointers can be used in team meetings if you are training a group of people who work together or sent back to individual work settings for discussion in team meetings if the participants are from a variety of work settings.

• Allow about 10 minutes for summing up. Ask each participant to say one point that they have learned from the day about working in partnership with service users and carers that they will take with them into their own practice.

Suggested Further Reading

Simons, K. (1999) *A Place at the Table? Involving People with Learning Difficulties in Purchasing and Commissioning Services.* Kidderminster, British Institute of Learning Disabilities.

Thomas, J. (2006) *Understanding and Supporting Professional Carers*, Oxford, Radcliffe Publishing.

Thompson, N. (2007) *Power and Empowerment*, Lyme Regis, Russell House Publishing.

Voluntary Action Westminster (2006) *Involving People: A Practical Guide.* www.vswcvs.org/uploads/involving-people-a-practical-guide.pdf

Warren, J. (2007) *Service User and Carer Participation in Social Work*, Exeter, Learning Matters.

Webb, R. and Tossell, D. (1998) *Social Issues For Carers: Towards Positive Practice*, 2nd edn, London, Hodder Arnold.

Legal and Moral Issues

Setting the scene

Given the complexity of both of these concepts, you will have to be realistic about what can be covered in the time you will have available. Our aim in what follows is just to remind those working with adults that they work within legal and moral contexts which cannot be ignored, and to promote discussion about the implications of this for their practice with vulnerable people. While there is unlikely to be an expectation on those human services workers who are attending the course to be legal experts, we would suggest that there is an expectation that they have a reasonable understanding of the law relating to their specific areas of responsibility and at least a basic awareness and understanding of the overarching pieces of legislation (for example, those concerned with human rights, discrimination and so on) that can make a positive difference to powerless individuals or groups. Doel and Shardlow (2005) use the term 'law-informed practice' when referring to the need for social work students to be 'as aware of what they don't know as of what they do know' [p.219] and we would want to extend this expectation to all of those working with adults in the broad field of human services. That is, it is important to be aware that there will be legal or moral issues that will govern or affect their work and an expectation that they know about them, or at least know how to get that information when it is needed. The law has the potential to both constrain and empower and the exercises which follow are designed to get people thinking about how this affects the particular work they do, or would like to do.

We have included a focus on moral issues because people work is characterised by dilemmas. There will always be conflicting perspectives on what is the 'right' or 'wrong' approach to any matter, not just between individuals but at a cultural and societal level also. Because moral issues are often difficult to resolve, the tendency to avoid addressing them is tempting, and so we offer a few ideas for consciousness raising about the moral context of people work, which we hope will encourage further discussion and debate.

As the legal and moral context of people work underpins all aspects of practice, then it could be argued that any of the discussions in these three *Theory into Practice* books could provide food for thought in this area. However, we would highlight the following in particular:

Community Care: There are relevant discussions in Chapter 3 on partnership, in Chapter 4 on the right to take risk, in Chapter 7 on regulation and accountability and on equality assurance in Chapter 10.

Safeguarding Adults: Given that this book is based on the premise of vulnerability and protection from abuse and exploitation, and the judgement at a societal level that this is the right thing to do, the whole book could be said to provide food for thought. However, Chapter 3 has a particular focus on the legal and policy context.

Age Discrimination: Again, the whole book is based on a moral argument that discrimination on the grounds of age needs to be challenged at more than an individual level if significant numbers of adults are not to be disempowered or pushed to the margins of society.

Are We 'Law Informed'?

Aim

This is an exercise designed to help participants explore and build on their knowledge of key pieces of legislation and their understanding of its relevance to their practice - that is, to help them become more 'law informed' as referred to on page 25.

Materials

Three sheets of flip chart paper, the first headed 'Care Standards Legislation', the second 'Anti-Discrimination Legislation' and the third 'Health and Safety Legislation'; three coloured markers; white board or flip chart for recording feedback.

Timing

Allow about an hour for this exercise.

Notes for trainer

It may be that some participants respond with comments such as: 'We have a legal department, so I don't need to think about such matters'. In the face of that we would encourage you to respond by suggesting that engaging with this exercise is nevertheless useful, in that it will hopefully convince them that the legal context is something that they do need to think about, not only because of the positive opportunities it can offer in terms of empowering or protecting vulnerable adults, but also themselves as employees.

Activity

• This is a group exercise, but the group needs to be large enough to be divided into three smaller groups.

• Begin by dividing the main group into three smaller ones and issue each with one of the prepared sheets of flip chart paper and a marker pen (5 minutes).

• Ask each group to write, on their flip chart paper, anything they know about the area of legislation they have been allocated - for example, why it is important to what they do. After about 15 minutes, take the flip chart from the first group and pass it to the second, giving that group's flip chart paper to the third group who, in turn, will pass theirs on to the first group, so that each group now has a different piece of paper and a different area of law to consider.

• Now ask each group to look at what has already been written and make their own contribution to that record. Tell them that they can comment on what another group has written, or add to it, but they must not change or remove any comments that the previous group has made. Allow about 10 minutes for this stage.

Exercise 3.1. cont.

• Now move the papers around again and ask the participants to repeat the process once more – that is, to read and comment on what is already there and add any further thoughts they have but not to change or remove anything. Allow about 5 minutes for this stage.

• Pass the papers from group to group one more time. When the papers are passed on this time they should be back with the group which started them off. The task of each group now is to revisit their original comments and use what others have written to reinforce or add to their own learning and maybe to raise an agenda for future training or private study. The groups may appreciate being given the opportunity to look again at all three flip chart sheets, if they can be displayed somewhere in the room or made available in some way. Allow about 10 to 15 minutes for this final stage of reflection.

Exercise 3.2.

The Law as an Ally

Aim

This exercise is designed to get participants thinking about how the law can empower and protect as well as constrain and prohibit, and to think through the consequences for powerless and uninformed people if those with the potential to help do not use or refer to the powerful legal tools at their disposal.

Materials

Copies of the worksheet - Law-informed Practice - The Law as an Ally (you may want to separate them out so that each group receives just one case study); paper and pens; white board or flip chart for recording feedback.

Timing

Allow about an hour for this exercise.

Notes for trainer

If you feel that the group you are working with cannot be expected to know about the areas of law discussed, you might want to use the scenarios as a basis for joint discussion, rather than as exercises.

Activity

• This involves exploring case studies and so could be used for small group work or individual study.

• Spend a few minutes explaining that you want the participants to think about the potential for the law to empower vulnerable adults. Explain that they do not have to worry about being specific about the law concerned – an awareness that the law could help in some way will suffice if they don't know the details. Distribute a copy of the worksheet to each participant (about 5 minutes).

• Ask them to pair up or break off into small groups and work their way through the three scenarios. We would suggest allowing 10 to 15 minutes for each one – time prompts may be needed to ensure that all three are discussed.

• Ask the participants to return to the main group and invite feedback about how they think the law could help vulnerable people in those situations and, where its potential is not known or acted on, the consequences for missed opportunities for growth and change.

Law-informed Practice - The Law as an Ally

Study A

Sunita had already completed the first term of a performing arts course at her local college. Her tutors were aware that she had a mild learning disability and she had told them from the outset that she had impaired vision and epilepsy. Nothing had prevented her from engaging in all aspects of the course this far and she had made exellent progress. However, when she returned from her Christmas break she was told that she would not be allowed to complete the second term because it involved a circus skills component. They told her that they had responsibilities to fulfil in terms of health and safety legislation and, because they could not guarantee her safety, were having to prohibit her from taking part. Sunita was devastated because she would not be able to graduate without achieving a pass mark in all of the course modules and angry that she had not been told about this from the outset. She now felt that she would have to rethink her future and, feeling very despondent, went to tell Siwan from the advocacy project that she was having to give up her dream. Siwan, who had helped her to develop her skills and confidence enough to apply in the first place, had other ideas.

In what way(s), if any, could the law be helpful here in terms of Sunita's future?

What does this tell us about the importance of having an awareness, and at least a basic understanding, of the legal context of our work and the policies which arise from it?

Study B

Karen from the care agency had just left Arthur's house after her usual afternoon visit to help him prepare something for his tea and, because he had a degree of dementia, made sure he had remembered to take the medication he needed for his heart complaint. While she was there, she noticed that there was very little food in the house and, when she offered to get some for him, he told her that he had no money. Karen reminded him that she had only collected his pension for him the day before and so he should have had plenty of money for food. At this point, Arthur told her that he had given all his pension money to his grandson who had told him he needed money for petrol. Karen told her manager, who looked into this further, and they found out that the grandson and his friends were calling on Arthur every few days, pleading poverty and taking what money he had in his wallet. Karen and her manager were convinced that Arthur was the victim of financial abuse, and as such, in need of protection. However, Arthur didn't see it that way – he said he was happy to help out the only family member who ever took the time to visit him. They could see that he had rights, but worried that his judgment was impaired because of his dementia. Could he be forced to stop giving his money away if it was against his own interests?

In what way(s), if any, could the law be helpful here in terms of Arthur's future?

What does this tell us about the importance of having an awareness, and at least a basic understanding, of the legal context of our work and the policies which arise from it?

Study C

Irene had borne the brunt of Jack's temper and frustration for most of their 44 years of married life. He had often been violent towards her but Irene had chosen to stay in the relationship because she loved him, and the times when he wasn't under the influence of drugs or alcohol and threatening to or actually harming her, were good times in her opinion and made up for the bad. However, over the past few years, Jack had become chronically ill because of kidney and liver problems and used emotional pressure to dissuade Irene from leaving him. Irene had her own problems struggling to manage her life with bipolar disorder. She reached a particularly low point when he destroyed treasured photographs and, having had enough, she moved out of their house and went to stay with a friend. With her friend's emotional support, she sought the advice of some-one at a Women's Aid centre in a nearby town. When Jack found out, he was furious and began making threatening phone calls and sending friends of his to the place she was staying at, to tell Irene that he would harm her and her family and friends if she didn't return to do her 'duty' as the carer of a sick husband.

In what way(s), if any, could the law be helpful here in terms of Irene's future?

What does this tell us about the importance of having an awareness, and at least a basic understanding, of the legal context of our work and the policies which arise from it?

Exercise 3.3.

Facing Dilemmas

Aim

When working with adults who need help we often face dilemmas – life is complicated and no-one ever said people work would be easy! This exercise highlights the fact that dilemmas need to be recognised as such before problem-solving strategies can be sought.

Materials

Copies of the worksheet - Facing Dilemmas; paper and pens; white board or flip chart for recording feedback.

Timing

Allow about an hour to an hour and a half for this exercise.

Activity

• Suitable for small group work or individual study.

• After explaining the purpose of the exercise, ask the participants to break off into small groups and consider the case studies on the worksheet that you hand out to them (about 5 minutes). Allow about 15 to 20 minutes of discussion time for each scenario – you may need to give time prompts to move on to look at all three (about 45 to 60 minutes). If you have time, you may want to invite detailed feed back but the exercise will have served its purpose if you can be satisfied from the feedback that the participants recognise that, in many situations, there is no 'right' answer, and that seeking help in those situations is a mark of good practice (10 to 20 minutes).

Facing Dilemmas

Study A

For three years Cassie had been helping Jackie to have a say in matters that affected her day to day life. Jackie had a learning disability and severe communication difficulties and Cassie got to know her when she become involved in an advocacy scheme which links those who have difficulty making their voice heard with others who have the confidence and skills to facilitate this. When Cassie had attended a workshop at the beginning of the relationship, it had been made clear that her role was merely to act as a mouthpiece for Jackie - someone to say what Jackie would say if she had the ability to do so. Cassie had always tried to respect that and had not made decisions for her or even tried to influence Jackie when she had not agreed with her. She respected Jackie's right to make her own decisions but was concerned when it became clear that she was intending to sign over to her brother her share of a house they had inherited from their parents. Cassie felt that the brother was being unscrupulous, but Jackie was happy with his explanation that he was 'saving her from having to worry about stuff'. Things came to a head when Jackie asked her to help her sort matters out with a solicitor.

What was the nature of Cassie's dilemma or dilemmas?

What might you have done in her position?

Who could you have discussed the dilemma(s) with or turned to for support?

Study B

Elsa had been in poor health for many years but had become increasingly reliant on Joe, her husband, after suffering from a severe bout of pneumonia on top of everything else. Although Joe was himself unwell, suffering from heart disease and chronic breathing problems, he insisted that he could look after Elsa's needs without any outside help, even though that entailed lifting her in and out of bed and on and off the toilet several times a day. Alan, a care manager, had spent many visits trying to persuade Joe that their quality of life would improve if he allowed himself to be relieved of at least some of the care tasks he took on alone. But Joe would have none of it – his argument was that they had managed their own affairs for all sixty-eight years of their time together and they weren't about to change that now. Much as Alan worried about the consequences of this decision for both Joe and Elsa, he had no reason to suspect that their reasoning was compromised in any way and so chose to respect their right to live in the manner of their own choosing, even though he suspected that the likelihood of both of them dying soon as a consequence were high. Alan was aware that Elsa and Joe's son, who lived over a hundred miles away, was putting pressure on them to get help or move into a home, as was their GP. He too had received several calls from the surgery, insisting that he act on his duty to protect such vulnerable people.

What was the nature of Alan's dilemma or dilemmas?

What might you have done in his position?

Who could you have discussed the dilemma(s) with or turned to for support?

Study C

Jimmy's work at a homeless people's project brought rewards as well as disappoint-ments. He had worked hard to establish a good working relationship with the local housing department, health centre and tenants' association and always felt proud of the part he had played when someone who wanted a secure home managed to achieve that aim. He had felt that way when Darren had been offered the tenancy of a new flat and felt confident that Darren's new-found sense of security and optimism would have a positive impact on his long-standing mental health problems. For the first few months Darren took a pride in his new property and his outlook on life was very positive – he signed up for a course at his local college and began eating well and looking after him-self generally. However, after this initial period, Jimmy noticed a sharp decline in Darren's appearance and demeanour and began receiving calls from the police who were regularly being called to the premises by neighbours who were fed up with the loud music and abusive language coming from Darren's flat at all hours of the day and night. Jimmy suspected that Darren's brother and his friends were taking advantage of Darren's low self-esteem and lack of assertiveness by treating his accommodation as their own. This was confirmed when he visited and found several people in the flat taking drugs. He offered to get help to evict Darren's uninvited 'house guests' but Darren begged him not to as he feared the consequences.

What was the nature of Jimmy's dilemma or dilemmas?

What might you have done in his position?

Who could you have discussed the dilemma(s) with or turned to for support?

Exercise 3.4.

A Question of Values

Aim

We include this exercise about exploring values because, where values conflict, dilemmas often follow.

Materials

Copies of the Worksheet - A Question of Values, white board or flip chart for recording feedback.

Timing

Allow about 30 to 40 minutes for this exercise.

Note for trainer

In our efforts to offer resources for a very broad ranging readership, the questions we have posed on the worksheet are of a general nature. You may want to substitute others of your own design in order to tailor it more specifically to a particular group's experience. What matters is that they are worded in a way that requires participants to think about their own value base and how it might conflict with the value base of others (including an organisation's value base). Choose statements that are likely to highlight differences so that they are likely to raise dilemmas about competing perspectives.

Activity

• As it uses a worksheet format it is suitable for small group work or individual study.

• Ask participants to work through the worksheet - A Question of Values, on their own and then bring the group together to discuss how what we think affects what we do (or do not do) and the implications of this for whatever field of practice we work in with vulnerable adults.

A Question of Values

Have a look at the following statements and make brief notes about whether you agree or disagree with the values that underpin them.

When someone becomes dependent, care by the family is always the best option.

I agree/disagree because

Although the views of service users and carers do matter, the breadth of experience that professionals can bring makes their input more important.

I agree/disagree because

Vulnerable adults must be protected, even if it isn't what they want.

I agree/disagree because

Communities are where we feel safe and valued, so community care is bound to be a good policy.

I agree/disagree because

Once you become old you should not expect to live as full and varied a life as you have done previously.

I agree/disagree because

We're all the same under our skin, so there shouldn't be separate initiatives for people from different ethnic groups.

I agree/disagree because

Suggested Further Reading

Banks, S. (2006) *Ethics and Values in Social Work*, 3rd edn, Basingstoke, Palgrave Macmillan.

Bernard, M. and Scharf, T. (eds) (2007) *Critical Perspectives on Ageing Societies*, Bristol, The Policy Press.

Clements, L. and Thompson, P. (2007) *Community Care and the Law,* 4th edn, London, Legal Action Group Education and Service Trust.

Hughes, J. and Baldwin, C. (2006) *Ethical Issues in Dementia Care: Making Difficult Decisions*, London, Jessica Kingsley.

Moss, B. (2007) *Values*, Lyme Regis, Russell House Publishing.

Puri, B.K., Brown, R.A., Mckee, H.J. and Treasden, I.H. (2005) *Mental Health Law: A Practical Guide*, London, Hodder Arnold.

Ridout, P. (ed) (2003) *Care Standards: A Practical Guide*, Bristol, Jordan Publishing.

Watson, J. and Woolf, M. (2003) *Human Rights Act Toolkit*, London, Legal Action Group Education and Service Trust.

Listening Skills

Setting the scene

Listening skills are discussed in *Age Discrimination* and *Community Care*.

Listening is a key skill in social care. It sounds straightforward, but it is in fact a very complex process. Listening is a skill which most people probably think they are good at. However, when service users have been consulted, they have said that they are not always listened to (Koprowska, 2005). It is possible for human services workers to think they are listening to service users, but they do not accurately hear what is said or for some reason choose not to hear what is said. It is not really possible to work in an anti-discriminatory way without listening to service users. The reason for this is that human services workers cannot understand the needs, experiences and perspectives of service users without taking on board what they have to say. Without accurate listening, human services workers act on their own assumptions about service users and their needs, and this can lead to their supporting them in ways which are oppressive, even if this is not the intention. This session is designed to explore the process of listening and what helps and hinders 'good' listening.

Lessons from Experience

Aim

This is a creative exercise, designed to enable participants to think about the emotions and frustrations caused by someone not listening to them.

Materials

A sheet of flip chart paper and some pens for each group; Blutack or similar for putting results on wall (if allowed).

Timing

Allow about an hour for this exercise.

Notes for trainer

Participants might need some reassurance about doing this exercise, as some find it easier to write things down or talk about them. Give reassurance that there is no right or wrong way of doing this and that it is a chance to work in a different way.

Activity

- Individual and small group work.

- Ask each participant to think of a time when they really felt that they were not being listened to. Explain that this has to be an example that they are willing to share with the group. Allow about 5 minutes for this.

- Once everyone has thought of an example, ask people to get into small groups of 4 or 5 people. Ask each group to share with each other their examples of how each of them felt when they weren't listened to. Allow about 10 minutes for this.

- Once this has been done give each group a piece of flip chart paper and felt tip pens or flip chart pens. Ask each group to represent visually the emotions they have talked about. Allow about 30 minutes for this.

- Ask each group to display their work, so that everyone has an opportunity to walk around and view what other groups have produced. Allow about 10 minutes for this or longer if participants want to discuss what they have produced or seen.

Top 10 Barriers to Listening to Service Users

Aim

The first exercise should provide a basis for the rest of the session. The groups will have produced work that represents very powerfully what it feels like to not be listened to. Explain that service users often feel that they are not listened to and sometimes this is the result of human services workers not being fully aware of what can affect the way they listen to them. The purpose of this exercise is to explore the listening process.

Age Discrimination (p. 37) identifies a number of distractions that can get in the way of someone listening. This exercise encourages participants to think of their own working environment and to identify what can stop them listening to a service user.

Explain that in the next exercise you are going to explore ways to try and prevent service users feeling the way that the posters from the first exercise show.

Materials

Paper and pens or flip chart sheets and marker pens.

Timing

Allow 30 to 45 minutes for this exercise.

Activity

• Small group work.

• Ask people to get into groups of about 4 or 5 people. Ask each group to produce a list of the top 10 things that happen that stop them listening to service users and then to prioritise them. Examples might be not having enough staff due to sickness, being too tired or being called away to do something else. Allow 15 minutes for this and then ask each group to share their lists. Point out any common themes and say that you will return to these points at the end of the session.

Listening Case Study

Aim

This exercise is based around the statement on why listening is crucial in *Age Discrimination* (p. 37):

> 'It gives us a perspective on how other people define the problem to be addressed'.

Although this statement was about age discrimination it holds true for working with all adults (and indeed children and young people).

Materials

Copies of Case Study 6; paper and pens for each group; white board or flip chart for recording feedback.

Timing

45 minutes plus an extra 15 minutes per group and a further few minutes for drawing together.

Notes for trainer

At the end of this case study it will be clear that June did not develop any understanding at all of how Mavis might define the 'problem' or even of what the 'problem' might be.

Activity

- Work in pairs or small groups with the case study as a focus.

- Ask participants to read Case Study 6. In pairs or small groups, ask them to answer the questions at the end of the case study. In addition to being made available at the end of this part, the questions are reproduced here with some points to help with taking feedback from the group. Allow 45 minutes for the case study, reading and answering the questions in small groups and a further 15 minutes for each group feeding back.

1. **June fails to talk to Mavis when she said she would. If she was having difficulty in finding time to talk to her, what should she have done differently?**

June should have been more realistic when she told Mavis when she would speak to her. If she was having difficulty finding the time to see her, she should have gone back to her and negotiated another time to see her.

2. **June went to talk to Mavis in the lounge. What is the problem with this and what do you think she should have done?**

The lounge was not a private area and June had assumed that it was all right to talk to Mavis there, although she didn't know what she wanted to talk to her about. June should have asked her where she wanted to talk to her and offered to talk to her away from other people.

3. **June assumed that Mavis was developing dementia as she couldn't understand her behaviour. Why do you think she assumed this and what questions do you think she should be asking herself?**

June was making an ageist assumption and had no reason to assume that Mavis might be affected by dementia other than she could not account for her behaviour. The key thing here is that June didn't question what she had done but immediately thought something was amiss with Mavis. June should have been asking herself what else might account for Mavis's behaviour and whether there was anything that she might have done which could be triggering the mysterious behaviour.

4. **June lets Mavis down again in the dining room. While you might understand her reasons, what effect do you think this could have on Mavis?**

Mavis could be getting frustrated by this time, as June hasn't listened to her. Mavis has something important to tell June and the danger is that she may not be able to tell her about her concerns.

5. **June talks to Mavis in her bedroom while Mavis is getting dressed. What should June have done differently in this situation?**

As Mavis is getting dressed, it is not a good time to talk to her, as this is not respecting her privacy. Also, she has her back to Mavis, so Mavis cannot hear June, which is bad practice for two reasons: firstly because she has no eye contact with her which is important in communication and secondly because it makes it difficult for Mavis to hear her.

6. **June does eventually meet with Mavis, but Mavis gives up with the idea of telling her about Bill. What impact do you think this could have on Mavis and Bill?**

Mavis may well not report any concerns in the future. She may well have got the message that her needs are not June's primary concern. Bill doesn't know anything about what has happened but is affected, as no one will now support him in what could well be an instance of financial abuse.

• Take feedback on each question, starting with a different group for each question and then asking if any other groups want to add anything. The overall point to be made in the feedback is that, although a lot of what happens is understandable, the end result is that Mavis is not listened to at all and Bill is left with a situation which might be abusive. Although June does not intend any disrespect to Mavis or would not ignore the concern about Bill if she knew about it, her behaviour in this case study has the effect of shutting down the channels of communication and Mavis is not listened to.

Active Listening

Aim

So far the session has explored issues of when communication doesn't go well because the service user is not listened to. Thompson (2002) states:

> Perhaps the most important point to emphasize is that listening is an *active* process. It involves not only hearing what is said, but also indicating to the other person that we have heard it. This provides reassurance for the speaker and encourages him or her to speak freely and openly. (p. 89)

Thompson then identifies what active listening involves:

- Acknowledging feelings;
- Appropriate use of body language;
- Resisting the temptation to interrupt;
- Paying careful attention to what is being said, to avoid misunderstandings;
- Avoiding jumping to conclusions or relying on stereotypes; and
- Reflecting back key points of what has been said, to confirm understanding.

This exercise will explore the listening process and stress the importance of 'active listening'.

Materials

Copies of the worksheet - Active Listening; paper and pens; white board or flip chart for recording feedback.

Timing

Allow about an hour for this exercise.

Activity

- This is a role play activity with participants working in groups of three.

- For this exercise, ask participants to get into threes. Then give each member of the group of three a role as reproduced in the worksheet. Ask the participant who plays the service user to do the role play twice, the first time with Support Worker 1 while Support Worker 2 watches and then stop them after 5 or 10 minutes where the scenario is re-enacted with Support Worker 2, while Support Worker 1 watches. As with the first role play, let it go on for 5 or 10 minutes.

• After the role plays have finished, ask the members of each group to discuss how each role play went and to highlight the differences between the two support workers and what difference their varied approaches made to how the service user felt.

• Take feedback from each group and discuss with the whole group the value of active listening and highlight to the group the characteristics of active listening as cited from Thompson. Pay particular attention to the reflecting back of key points about what is being said and ask Support Worker 2 how they managed to do this. Then ask the service users in the role plays to say if this made them feel listened to.

• Refer back to the first exercise and remind the group of the feelings they represented visually. These feelings resulted from being not listened to. Explain to the group that these feelings are often the result of the frustrations caused by discrimination, but this should not be regarded as occurring merely on a personal level.

Active Listening

Service user

You are a service user who is very upset about something which has happened to you. You want to tell your support worker all about it, but need a lot of encouragement, as you find it difficult to talk about it.

Support worker 1 (Not good at listening support worker)

You are the support worker to the service user in this exercise. The service user wants to tell you about something that has happened to them but you have the following characteristics:

- You interrupt

- You don't acknowledge how the service user is feeling

- You jump to conclusions about what the service user is saying

- You misunderstand what they are saying

Support Worker 2 (An active listening support worker)

You are the support worker for the service user in this exercise. The service user wants to tell you about something that has happened to them. Listen to them using the following:

- Acknowledge how they are feeling

- Don't interrupt them

- Pay attention to what the service user says

Mirror what the service user says to you by checking out that your understanding is correct.

Suggested Further Reading

Burley Allen, M. (1995) *Listening: The Forgotten Skill: A Self-Teaching Guide*, New Jersey, John Wiley.

Koprowska, J. (2005) *Communication and Interpersonal Skills in Social Work,* Exeter, Learning Matters.

Moss, B. (2007) *Communication Skills For Health and Social Care*, London, Sage.

Thompson, N. (2002) *People Skills*, 2nd edn, Basingstoke, Palgrave Macmillan.

Thompson, N. (2003) *Communnication and Language*, Basingstoke, Palgrave Macmillan.

Trevithick, P. (2005) *Social Work Skills: A Practice Handbook,* 2nd edn, Maidenhead, Open University Press.

Rights and Risks

Setting the Scene

Community Care and *Age Discrimination* both discuss managing risk. The consideration of risk and rights has never been more relevant than it is today. There is growing emphasis on risk assessment and also on not restricting service users' rights. It is possible to overemphasise either rights or risk in isolation, whereas they need to be considered together. So, this session is concerned with the two concepts which are considered together. To consider one without the other can lead to oppressive or dangerous practice. Social care is a very complex area of work where the rights of individuals are very often balanced against risks to either themselves or others. The approach of human services workers to risk taking can have a profound influence on the experience of the adults they support and can either promote or deny them their rights.

What is Risk?

Aim

In this exercise the participants are asked to explore the concept of risk and how it can be conceptualised in different ways.

Materials

Paper and pens; white board or flip chart for recording feedback.

Timing

Allow about 30 minutes for this exercise.

Activity

• This is suitable for small group work or working in pairs.

• By way of an introduction to this exercise, have a whole group discussion about what risk is. Ask participants to discuss a definition of risk in pairs and then ask them to share their definitions with the whole group. Allow 10 minutes for the work in pairs. Write key words or phrases on a white board or flip chart. Look at the list of words and phrases you have on the flip chart and ask the group whether risk looks positive or negative from this list. Does the list suggest 'danger' or 'opportunity'? It may be that the list suggests both. Make the point to the group that the way that risk is viewed is important, as it can be a defining factor in how people practise.

Risk as Part of Everyday Life

Aim

This exercise is designed to start participants thinking of risk taking in their own lives. The reason for this is to encourage an understanding that risk taking is an essential part of everyday life without which life would be poorer.

Materials

Flip chart paper and marker for each group; white board or flip chart for recording feedback.

Timing

Allow about an hour for this exercise.

Activity

• This involves individual thinking time and small group work.

• Ask each participant to think of a time in their life when they took a risk. Give some examples of taking a risk that are fairly common, such as the risk of starting a new job, moving house, taking up a sport, starting a new personal relationship.

• Ask participants to think of a risk that they are happy to share with the rest of the group. Allow people a minute or two to think of an example and then ask them to get into groups of four or five people. Ask each group member to share their example with the rest of their small group. Once the examples are shared, ask each group to pick an example from the group. Next ask the group to think of a list of five reasons why this example might have been too risky a venture for the person to have undertaken. Give some examples to explain what you mean: for a sport, the person might get injured, for a holiday, they could lose their passport abroad or for a relationship, it might not work out and the person could get hurt.

• Ask the groups to spend about 10 minutes listing reasons against the person embarking on that particular venture as it is 'too risky'. Ask each group to feed back on their list and ask the person whose example was selected to say what they thought of the reasons put forward. You may get a mixture of responses depending on what has happened in each example, so some might agree with the list of reasons, whereas others may well disagree.

• To begin a whole group discussion, ask why it is important to be able to take risks in life. The participants should be able to tell you reasons, such as: to try new things, to do exciting things, to develop as a person and so forth. They might even say that it is their right to take risks, even if the venture does not work out as they hoped. It is important to consider the point that people have the right to take risks in their lives, and this includes service users.

Risks - Acceptable or Not?

Aim

The previous exercise should have helped the group establish that risk taking is a positive part of life for them as individuals. If this has not come out of the exercise clearly, introduce this exercise by discussing this issue with the main group. Once this principle has been established, it is time to move on to consider risks for adults who are supported to live their lives.

Materials

Copies of the worksheet - Risk Scenarios; paper or flip chart sheet and pens; white board or flip chart for recording feedback.

Timing

Allow about an hour for this exercise.

Activity

• Suitable for working in small groups but the worksheet could also be used as an aid to individual study.

• Ask groups of 4 or 5 to look at the risk scenarios reproduced in the worksheet, and for each scenario to answer the question: Are the risks in this situation acceptable or not? Allow 20 minutes for discussion and then discuss each scenario with the whole group. As part of the discussion ask what the potential benefits are, which could be balanced against the risk, and also what could happen if things go wrong? On balance, which scenarios present risks that the group think are acceptable and which are not. Ask the group what makes the difference to the way they think about the different activities. Is it the different situations or has it got anything to do with attitudes towards the individuals in each situation?

Risk Scenarios

Scenario 1

Josey is a young adult with a learning disability. She wants to go 'clubbing' with her friends in the city centre.

Scenario 2

Adnan is an adult who is a wheelchair user. He wants to take part in the sport of wheel-chair basketball. Adnan has always been excluded from sports, but is a very keen basketball fan.

Scenario 3

Joe is an older person who has dementia and has just moved to live in a residential home. He has asked if he can go to the papershop by himself, as this has always been an important part of his daily routine.

Scenario 4

Betty is an older person who has had a stroke. She has made a partial recovery but now needs assistance to help her walk, and has only partial use of one hand. Betty lives in a warden-aided flat where she lived before the stroke. Betty is very independent and particularly enjoys visiting her friend in a nearby town. Betty used to drive herself there and wants to continue to do so.

Exercise 5.4.

Planning to Minimise Risk

Aim

This exercise will use the scenarios from the previous exercise to explore the nature of planning for minimising risk. So far in the session a stance towards risk has been explored which promotes the positive aspects of risk as an essential part of people's lives and so part of their rights. *Community Care* (p. 9) states the importance of identifying precisely the nature of the risk rather than being vague about it. Without being precise it is impossible to develop a plan of action for minimising the risk. The purpose of this exercise is to further this theme and to reinforce the need for careful planning to enable this positive risk taking.

Materials

Copies of the worksheet - Risk Scenarios; paper or flip chart sheet and pens; white board or flip chart for recording feedback.

Timing

Allow about an hour for this exercise.

Activity

   • Suitable for working in small groups, but the worksheet could also be used as an aid to individual study.

   • Ask groups of 4 or 5 to look at two of the scenarios each. Ensure that all scenarios are covered between the groups. Ask the groups to list exactly what the risks are in each situation. For example, with Josey, rather than just saying 'she would be vulnerable', list specific risks, such as, 'without support Josey might not be able to cope with unwanted attention, and so could be subjected to sexual advances against her wishes'. Ask the groups to list as many specific risks in each situation as they can think of. Allow about 30 minutes for this to be completed.

   • Once the groups have their lists of risks for the two scenarios they are considering, ask them to look at them and to think of ways of minimising each of the risks – in other words to develop a plan. You might want to use Josey's situation as an example. If she finds it difficult to cope with unwanted attention she might be subjected to sexual advances against her wishes. Ways of minimising the risk might be:

1. Support to understand the risks which could include discussions and role play

2. Support to develop strategies to deal with unwanted attention

3. Someone of her own age to accompany Josey to the club for the first time she goes, and then to discuss how she coped and then to review what further support she might or might not need.

• This example might not have been the choice of strategies for minimising the risk that you or the group would have taken, but serves to show that the point of the exercise is to be precise.

• Before the groups start this exercise, ask them if the above 'plan' is specific enough to address the issue of this particular risk. If the group thinks that it is, ask them how points 1 and 2 are going to be carried out and by whom. The group might well spot this oversight and this should help them with this exercise. The plan should identify how each point should be carried out, when and by whom. In the plans that the groups draw up they can invent these parts of the plan, but it is important that their plans are detailed. Allow about 30 minutes for the task.

• Once the groups have completed their plans ask them to share them with the main group.

Exercise 5.5.

Risk and Practice

Aim

This is designed to move the group on from analysing the case study to thinking about their own practice.

Materials

Copies of the worksheet - Risk Scenarios; paper or flip chart sheet and pens; white board or flip chart for recording feedback.

Timing

Allow about 30 minutes for this exercise.

Activity

     • Further discussion in small groups.

     • Ask the whole group how they could apply this approach to the people they work with. Ask them to discuss this in pairs for ten minutes and then ask for feedback from the pairs.

Positive Risk Taking

Aim

In *Community Care* (p. 38), Thompson and Thompson state: 'A person's right to take risks is not absolute, but there has to be a good reason for another person to interfere in that right. This means that, in a community care context, we have to be careful not to interfere in a person's risk-taking behaviour without proper justification'. The main areas for this justification are then identified as being:

> • Where the person concerned is placing one or more people at risk of serious risk of harm.

> This may involve a criminal matter where one person's behaviour is endangering another – for example, where threatening behaviour is involved. However, such situations have to be weighed up very carefully.

> • Where, owing to a mental health problem, the individual concerned is placing him- or herself or other people at serious risk of harm.

The aim of this exercise is to encourage critical analysis of risk management.

Materials

White board or flip chart for recording feedback.

Timing

Allow about 20 minutes for whole group discussion.

Activity

> • This is designed as an activity for the participants as one main group.

> • As a whole group discussion, look at the four scenarios again and ask if any of those fit into the points for unacceptable risk-taking behaviour as outlined above. Participants might have different views about this issue but are most likely to identify scenario 4 as an example of unacceptable risk-taking behaviour. If this is the case, discuss with the group what would need to be done to test out whether Betty should continue driving or not. This would need an assessment which would not be by staff working with her but by her GP and by the relevant authorities. However, it is important to point out that ageist assumptions should not be made, as many people do recover from strokes and are as safe driving their cars as other people.

• Ask the participants to each state an area of positive risk taking which they think is important for the adults they support.

Suggested Further Reading

Carson, D. and Bain, A. (2008) *Professional Risk and Working with People: Decision Making in Health, Social Care and Criminal Justice*, London, Jessica Kingsley.

Kemshall, H. and Pritchard, J. (1995) *Good Practice in Risk Assessment and Risk Management* , London, Jessica Kingsley.

Kemshall, H. and Pritchard, J. (1997) *Key Themes for Protection, Rights and Responsibilities,* Vol 2, London, Jessica Kingsley.

Parsloe, P. (1999) *Risk Assessment in Social Care and Social Work*, London, Jessica Kingsley.

Thompson, N. and Thompson, S. (2007) *Understanding Social Care*, 2nd edn, Lyme Regis, Russell House Publishing.

Titterton, M. (2004) *Risk and Risk Taking in Health and Social Care*, London, Jessica Kingsley.

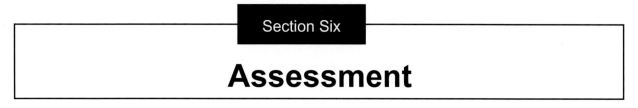

Assessment

Setting the Scene

Assessment is a really important topic because, without an accurate assessment, it is very difficult to meets the needs of service users. Assessment is one of the central tasks for those who work with and support adults. It is often reduced to a 'tick box' process which is unsatisfactory for both assessor and the person being assessed. This session will explore ways in which to assess service users in a more person-centred way and in a way which should tell the person being assessed that their view of their own needs is valid and essential to the process. It explores the concept of the 'expert' in assessment and highlights the expertise of service users in the process.

Assessment is discussed in *Community Care*.

What is Important to You?

Aim

This exercise is designed to get participants thinking about what is important in their lives and which they would want anyone on which they were dependent to be aware of. In this way they will be encouraged to begin to explore the importance of the process of assessment as a basis for care and support.

Materials

Flip chart paper and pen for each group; white board or flip chart for recording feedback.

Timing

Allow about an hour for this exericse.

Notes for trainer

When taking feedback from this exercise, make the point that assessment is concerned with people's everyday lives which includes their needs but should also include how they prefer to have their needs met. This does not just mean what service they want but what is important to them about how they are supported.

Activity

• Individual and small group work.

• Ask the group to work individually for the first part of this exercise. Ask participants to imagine the following situation: they are going into hospital to have an operation which, as a side effect, will render them unable to talk for a couple of weeks. After the operation they are going to stay in a residential home to recover. Ask each participant to make a list of what they want the staff at the residential home to know about them so that they can make their life as near to 'normal' as possible. Allow about 10 minutes.

• Once people have done this individually, ask them to work in pairs or small groups to compare notes on what each has said and then to try and categorise their list into headings. Allow about 20 minutes.

• Ask each pair or small group to feedback to the main group what they have for their headings. They may have listed headings such as routines, food preferences, hobbies, preferred clothing or religious observations, depending on the group. About 10 minutes should be sufficient.

• Now ask the group to think about the way people they work with are assessed. Are they assessed according to what matters to the individuals in this group? What are the differences? Allow about 20 minutes for this discussion.

The Exchange Model

Aim

Community Care discusses the exchange model of assessment. In Exercise 6.1, participants were asked to think about what they would want people who were supporting them to know. The participants are experts in themselves and in the same way, service users and carers are experts in knowing about themselves and the way they like to be supported.

Community Care (p. 60) cites Smale (1993) as fully explaining the exchange model and summarises it as assuming that:

People

• are expert in themselves

The worker

• has expertise in the process of problem solving with others;
• understands and shares perceptions of problems and their management;
• gets agreement about who will do what to support whom;
• takes responsibility for arriving at the optimum resolution of problems within the constraint of available resources and the willingness of participants to contribute.

The first exercise is an introduction to thinking about this model in terms of vulnerable adults.

Materials

Copies of Case Study 7; paper or flip chart sheet and pens; white board or flip chart for recording feedback.

Timing

Allow about an hour for this exercise.

Activity

• This is designed for small group work but individuals could use the case study as an aid to study.

• For this exercise, ask the participants to read Case Study 7 and in small groups answer the questions set below it. The questions are framed to get participants to think about the process of assessment. Allow 40 minutes for the groups to answer the questions.

• The first question asks what problems there are that need to be solved. This is asking participants to think about the situation as a whole in terms of Harjit's needs and wishes and whether he can live in his own flat, but also in terms of the opposition of his foster carers.

• The second question is asking what the priorities should be in solving these problems. This is where the idea of a process of working with Harjit and his foster carers should start to develop. Participants may well think of different steps that they would take in working with Harjit, but they should include:

> – Talking with Harjit to see how he views his future;
> – Talking with Harjit about his needs and how he thinks these can be met in his own flat;
> – Talking to Harjit about his foster carers' views and how he wants them to be included in the assessment process;
> – Talking to the foster carers either with Harjit or on their own, depending on what Harjit has told you he wants to happen, about his needs and also addressing their concerns;
> – Once the assessment is completed, exploring different options with Harjit.

• The third question asks how the participants would ensure that Harjit's expertise on himself was valued in assessing his needs and circumstances. This is asking about the approach that should be taken with Harjit and participants may suggest asking open questions or asking Harjit to talk about himself and his strengths and support needs or asking him to write about himself. The point here is that Harjit should be respected as the expert on himself and the assessor should look for a way of facilitating Harjit in the telling of his story and his strengths, needs, wishes and fears in his own way.

• The fourth question asks how the foster carers could be included in the assessment. This will depend on what Harjit has said he wants to happen, but this may need some discussion with him about different ways of doing this and what he feels most comfortable with. The foster carers have cared for Harjit for a long time, so will have a valuable role to play in the assessment process. It is also an important relationship for Harjit and one which he wants to maintain, so this makes working with them in a positive way even more important.

• Ask the groups to feed back their discussion. Ask a different group to feed back on each question, then ask if the other groups have anything to add.

Assessment and Partnership

Aim

This activity has a focus on how the assessment process can be carried out in a spirit of partnership.

Materials

Copies of Case Study 7; paper or flip chart sheet and pens; white board or flip chart for recording feedback.

Timing

Allow about an hour for this exercise.

Activity

• This is designed for small group work but individuals could use the case study as an aid to study.

• Ask participants to work in small groups and to think in more detail about asking Harjit to talk about himself and his strengths and needs. Ask the groups to make a list of all the things the assessor would need to know about Harjit to form a true view of his strengths and needs and what support he might need to live independently in a flat. Once they have completed the list, ask them to discuss how they can find out these details without resorting to a questioning style with Harjit. The questioning style casts the worker as the expert, which is not in the spirit of the exchange model. Allow 30 minutes for this discussion.

• Facilitate discussion based on the feedback from the groups in relation to this question. Participants might think that it is difficult not to ask any questions, as Harjit might forget to tell them something important. The answer to this is that it is the approach that is important. It may be that it is necessary to prompt Harjit or ask him about specific details. The approach should be one of considering Harjit as the expert on himself rather than one of asking him detailed questions about what the assessor thinks are his needs.

Assessment Skills

Aim

This exercise is designed to continue the theme of assessing in partnership, but has more of a focus on skill development.

Materials

Copies of Case Study 7; paper or flip chart sheet and pens; white board or flip chart for recording feedback.

Timing

Allow about 40 minutes for this exercise.

Activity

• A role-play activity for working in pairs.

• Continuing with Case Study 7, ask participants to work in pairs for a role enactment. Ask each pair to decide who will take the role of Harjit and who will be the assessor. Ask each pair to act out the worker asking Harjit about himself for the purposes of assessment. Ask the pairs to work within the context of the exchange model where Harjit is seen as the expert on himself and where the worker does not adopt a questioning style but encourages Harjit to share his views of himself, his needs and his wishes for the future. Ask the pairs to swap over so that everyone has a turn at being the worker. Allow 20 minutes for this exercise. After 10 minutes ask the pairs to swap roles.

• Ask the pairs to feed back on how they found this exercise. Ask them what the strengths are about working in this way and what are the difficulties with it. If participants raise difficulties, discuss these as a whole group to try and address them. Make the point that there is no one perfect approach and that a partnership approach will need working at. However, this way of working will communicate to the people they work with that they are valued as experts on their own lives.

Notes for trainer

Alternative exercise

If it is important that the group you are training consider how to assess service users who might need a lot of support, ask them to consider how they would use this approach with someone with different needs – for example, someone who doesn't use verbal communication. It is imperative that participants see this as an approach that can be adopted with people with different needs. The worker would have to think about how to work along these lines, but in such a way as to meet the communication needs of the service users. In an example such as this the service user could communicate by drawing or using their own form of communication, or the worker could work with them using pictures. Ask that participants discuss this in pairs initially and then facilitate a whole group discussion where the pairs feed back on their discussion.

Exercise 6.5.

After Assessment, What Next?

Aim

This exercise is concerned with getting agreement about support that follows from an assessment.

Materials

Copies of Case Study 7; paper or flip chart sheet and pens; white board or flip chart for recording feedback.

Timing

Allow about 45 minutes for this exercise.

Activity

- An exercise in planning as a follow up to previous work.

- It will again use the case study of Harjit. Ask the pairs who have just been working together to choose one of enactments they have performed and to make a list of the needs that the Harjit who one of them was playing specified. Once they have made the list, ask each pair to write against each need who would be responsible for meeting that need and when this would happen. They can make up the people who are responsible for the purposes of this exercise. The list may look like this:

  – Harjit needs transport to take him to college - Harjit to book taxis for days he is at college.
  – Harjit needs support to assist him in cleaning his flat - personal assistant to support every Thursday evening.
  – Harjit needs support to cook his food - personal assistant to support every day at 5 o'clock.
  – Harjit needs support to budget for his shopping - personal assistant to support every Friday afternoon.

- Allow 30 minutes for this discussion. Ask participants to share how they found this exercise. It can be difficult to break down the assessment into individual needs like this, but without doing this it is very difficult to allocate responsibilities for support. The purpose of this exercise is to reinforce the need for clarification of responsibilities following on from an assessment.

72

Exercise 6.5. cont.

Final words

Following on from the last exercise ask the whole group to think of ways that Harjit's wishes and views can be considered in the allocation of responsibilities to different people to support him in meeting his needs. This will give participants the opportunity to think about the importance of working in the way that the exchange model suggests at every stage of the assessment process.

Suggested Further Reading

Department of Health (1991) *Care Management and Assessment: A Practitioner's Guide*, London, HMSO.

Meteyard, B. (1994) *The Community Care Assessment Casebook*, Lyme Regis, Russell House Publishing.

Milner, J . and O'Byrne, P. (2002) *Assessment in Social Work*, Basingstoke, Palgrave Macmillan.

Parker, J. and Bradley, G. (2007) *Social Work Practice: Assessment, Planning, Intervention and Review,* 2nd edn, Exeter, Learning Matters.

Smale, G. and Tuson, G. with Biehal, N. and Marsh, P. (1993) *Empowerment, Assessment, Care Management and the Skilled Worker*, London, HMSO.

Walker, S. and Beckett, C. (2003) *Social Work Assessment and Intervention*, Lyme Regis, Russell House Publishing.

Continuous Professional Development and Staff Care

Setting the scene

The exercises which follow are designed to highlight the significance of ongoing learning if we are to maximise our personal effectiveness and maintain the standards that our professional bodies, those who use our services, and we ourselves expect. While this is largely a matter of personal responsibility, this will prove very difficult to achieve if the culture within which we work is one that does not recognise it as an integral part of what we do or fails to offer the support or resources that facilitate learning. It is easy to become demoralised and defeatist about ongoing learning when we don't feel valued or where we feel that the often difficult nature of our work is not recognised or validated by our employers. For this reason, these exercises focus initially on learning and development, but then move on to explore staff care more generally. Both of these topics merit much more attention than we are able to cover here, but we hope that they will serve as a springboard for getting these very significant topics on the agenda for further discussion.

These issues cross all boundaries in terms of working with adults because they relate to doing the best job possible in situations that are highly likely to be characterised by powerlessness, disadvantage and vulnerability. In relation to the publications in question, you might find it useful to refer back to the following discussions in:

Community Care: the need to keep up to date with political and, more specifically, social policy developments; understanding of legal duties; knowledge of resources; the development of critical thinking skills; user perspectives.

Safeguarding Adults: as above but, more particularly in terms of policy development and guidance, the discussions about mental capacity and recognising abuse; service user and carer feedback and its contribution to ongoing learning.

Age Discrimination: as above but also the need to understand the significance of anti-discriminatory values and to promote such initiatives; communication; multiple oppressions.

Staff development and staff care can both play an important part in helping to ensure that working with adults is fulfilling but, perhaps more importantly, they can also help to ensure that such practice is not 'dangerous' practice – that is, one which is not underpinned by sound knowledge and value bases and where skills are either absent, underdeveloped or misused because of a lack of understanding or a failure to keep up with new developments. As Thompson (2002) argues, a negative view of learning

'… could so easily pave the way for a form of routinized, uncritical practice'

(p. 71)

The following exercises should help to set participants thinking about the positive aspects of learning and encourage them to seek such support if they are not receiving it already.

Highlighting Learning

Aim

The aim of this exercise is to get participants thinking about the positives to be gained from valuing learning and being part of an environment where learning is valued.

Materials

Copies of the worksheet - New Learning; paper and pen; white board or flip chart for recording feedback.

Timing

Allow between 45 minutes and an hour for this exercise.

Notes for trainer

Where 'knowledge' is referred to, participants may need to be reminded that it is knowledge broadly defined. It could incorporate, for example, new information they have come across, techniques they have acquired or perspectives they have considered. Nor need it be confined to formal training or studying.

Activity

• This involves participants working in pairs to 'interview' each other about their recent learning.

• Ask the participants to team up with a partner and choose which of them is to act as interviewer and which to act as interviewee. Give each interviewer a copy of the worksheet. Ask each interviewee to identify some new knowledge they have picked up recently – this could be from reading, talking to a colleague, attending a training event or whatever. Allow 5 to 10 minutes.

• Having introduced the exercise and ensured that each pair has a focus, allow about 15 minutes or so for the questions on the worksheet to be worked through and the interviewer to make some notes. Then ask the partners to reverse roles (giving the new interviewer a copy of the worksheet), and repeat the interview with the new focus that person brings to the discussion. Allow a further 15 minutes.

• With the participants back together as one group invite feedback about what arose from their discussions – for example, whether they found it easy or difficult to identify what they had learned, whether they usually share what they have learned with other people and so on. It might be useful to have such questions ready as prompts.

• Spend 10 to 15 minutes with the whole group drawing out what has been learned from the task.

New Learning

1.   Who initiated the process of learning or acquiring the new knowledge?

2.   How useful could it potentially be for the work that you do?

3.   How will you incorporate this learning into your practice?

4.   Will you share this learning with others? If so, how?

New Learning

CPD - What Does it Mean?

Aim

Continuous professional development (CPD) is a commonly used term and refers to the need for individuals to see their working life as one of ongoing learning and an integration of learning and practice, rather than one where they can operate without engaging in learning once they have completed an induction period or qualifying training. Because it refers to such a wide-ranging concept as ongoing learning, there is often some confusion about what CPD means in specific circumstances. We have designed this exercise to get people thinking about their own situations and the importance that ongoing learning holds for them.

Materials

Sheets of paper and markers or pens; white board or flip chart for recording feedback.

Timing

Allow 45 to 90 minutes, depending on the size of the group.

Activity

• This is a group exercise which allows participants to explore the concept of CPD and what it means to them in their individual circumstances .

• Explain to the participants that you want them to use whatever form of expression they choose (as long as it isn't likely to offend anyone!) to express what the concept of continuous professional development means to them. They may choose to draw a basic picture or diagram, write something, use gestures or act out a (short) scenario – whatever they feel most comfortable with (about 5 minutes should be enough time for this introduction and to reassure people that they don't need to be Picasso or an Academy Award-winning actor). You need to plan ahead in terms of thinking about how much time the presentations are likely to take and, especially if the group is a large one, to ensure that there is enough time for everyone to make a contribution.

• When everyone has got something ready to say or do, invite them to share it with the rest of the group. Only do this when everyone is ready so that they will be able to give their full attention to the message others are giving. When everyone has had a turn (it would be advisable to try to ensure that this phase does not last so long that participants lose sight of the purpose of the exercise - we would suggest no longer than about 45 minutes), invite discussion about what emerged from this process. For example, were the representations predominantly positive or negative and, if so, what is this suggesting about CPD initiatives? Allow 10 to 15 minutes.

Exercise 7.2. cont.

• Draw the exercise to a close by drawing out the point that CPD incorporates many different types of learning and flagging it up as an important issue to address, especially if any of the feedback in the presentations has been negative. Allow about 10 to 15 minutes.

Evaluating CPD

Aim

Given that this exercise is about analysing the contribution that continuous professional development makes to practice, it provides an opportunity to raise its profile and help address any negativity surrounding it.

Materials

Copies of the worksheet - Lifelong Learning and a white board or flip chart to record feedback.

Timing

An hour may be enough, but we would suggest allowing some flexibility here, as some groups may need more time for reflection.

Notes for trainer

Some people can find it difficult at first to use the SWOT framework referred to below and may need some initial guidance. If it is something that you are unfamiliar with yourself and wish to read up on, the discussion in Thompson (2006a) is a useful starting point. We have included some guidance and suggestions for prompts and would advise that you circulate amongst the groups early on in the exercise in case some participants feel unconfident about what they are being asked to do.

Activity

• Designed for use in small groups, this worksheet-based activity can also be used by individuals in other settings.

• Introduce the exercise by explaining that SWOT analysis has been around for a long time and has its advocates in many different work environments. Add that it is being used here as a way of evaluating the usefulness of life-long learning and highlighting the difficulties that people can face when trying to incorporate it into their practice. Even if everyone claims to know what SWOT refers to, it is worthwhile reminding them that the 'strengths' and 'weaknesses' elements refer to the present, while the 'opportunities' and 'threats' elements refer to the future. Clarifying this should help to ensure that they are then clear about the task that follows. Allow 5 to10 minutes.

• Distribute a copy of the worksheet to each participant and ask them to go into pairs and help each other to work through a SWOT analysis of life-long learning and its implications for their practice (40 minutes) – it may take a little longer if people are not familiar with the technique and need time to 'settle in' to it.

• With the participants back as one group, draw out the positives and negatives that have emerged from the exercise and invite them to offer any tips and strategies they have found useful for maximising the opportunities for, and minimising the obstacles to, life-long learning/continuous professional development (20 minutes). If the feedback focuses heavily on obstacles to learning, it might be advisable to validate the importance of making CPD work for everyone and flag up the possibility of exploring that aspect more fully at another time. By doing so, the exercise should end on a note of promise, rather than negativity.

Lifelong Learning

Strengths	Weaknesses
Opportunities	**Threats**

Lifelong Learning (Trainer's Guidance)

Strengths

You could expect to see examples here of a range of knowledge, skills and values.

Prompt example:

What have you learned to date that has helped you to do your job well?

Weaknesses

Examples might include a lack of confidence; overwork; an anti-learning culture; a tendency to separate theory and practice.

Prompt example:

What might hold you back from learning, or act as a break on your learning?

Opportunities

Examples might include that it raises awareness of differing perspectives; being research minded helps to add a critical edge to one's thinking; keeping up to date with new strategies and approaches can enhance opportunities for change; it can win the respect of colleagues within and outside one's own discipline or profession.

Prompt example:

How can continuing to learn contribute to making your practice as effective as possible?

Threats

Threats could include the possibility of being taken off a professional register; that practice could become ineffective or even dangerous; loss of respect from colleagues and/or service users.

Prompt example:

What can go wrong or fail to happen if learning doesn't take place throughout your career?

Receiving Support

Aim

This activity is designed to help participants explore the circumstances in which they need support, and whether they get it, in the context of the emotionally demanding work they do.

Materials

Copies of the worksheet - Receiving Support; white board or flip chart for recording feedback.

Timing

Allow 75 to 90 minutes for this exercise.

Notes for Trainer

As this will require people to think about situations they have found difficult, it is important to anticipate heightened emotions and be sensitive to them. Finishing the plenary session with a focus on strategies can help to ensure that people don't go away from this activity feeling negative or demoralised.

Activity

• For the most part, this involves people working in pairs to interview each other using predefined questions.

• After explaining the purpose of this exercise, ask the participants to go into pairs and decide on who will act as interviewer and who will be interviewed. Issue each interviewer with a copy of the worksheet (5 to 10 minutes). Ask them to work through Part One with their partner, making very brief notes as they go along (about 15 minutes should suffice). When they have done so, ask them to swap over roles and revisit Part One of the worksheet so that the interviewer has the opportunity to be interviewed and vice versa. Allow another 15 minutes or so for this stage of the exercise.

• When both people have had a chance to talk through their negative experiences, ask them to revert to their original interviewer/interviewee status and work through Part Two of the worksheet, swapping roles after 15 minutes.

Exercise 7.4. cont.

• Finish the activity with a short discussion (10 to 20 minutes) in the main group about:

      – what has emerged as helpful;

      – what could have helped in situations where people felt hurt, demoralised or taken for granted; and

      – tips and strategies for getting support and feedback when it is needed.

Receiving Support

Part One

• Think back over the last few months or so and tell me about an experience you found enriching or rewarding, or a piece of work of which you were proud.

• Explain whether that success was validated or recognised in any way – were you congratulated, for example?

• How did you feel about that response (or lack of it)?

Part Two

• Think back over the last few months or so and tell me about an experience that was difficult or frustrating - perhaps involving a dilemma.

• Explain whether those difficulties were recognised and your experience taken seriously. Did you have the opportunity to discuss them with anyone, for example?

• How did you feel about this response (or lack of it)?

Evaluating Support

Aim

This exercise assumes that participants will be receiving support in some form or another from their managers. Formats could include formal supervision sessions, informal 'open door' style policies, mentoring schemes or whatever opportunity is offered for support and feedback.

Materials

Several pieces of 'Post-It' type notepaper for each participant, with access to more if needed and designated clear spaces, ideally a wall, door or board where notes can be placed for viewing.

Timing

Allow between 45 minutes and an hour for this exercise.

Notes for trainer

Participants may be reluctant to disclose negative experiences, and so it is advisable, before beginning, to reaffirm the ground rules concerning confidentiality. If you are taking on a trainer role with a group of people you also manage, you will need to gauge whether you and the group can deal with what emerges in a spirit of constructive criticism. If you decide to substitute it with a different exercise, then you might still find this one useful as a means of getting constructive feedback, but by asking your employees to complete the exercise individually and confidentially at another time.

Because this exercise is designed to raise negatives as well as positives and is likely to be the last exercise of the day, care needs to be taken to ensure that enough time is left to address the final question. If not, then there is the potential for the whole day to finish on a negative or demoralised note.

Activity

> • This calls for individuals to spend time thinking of positive and negative experiences of management support and feedback and then sharing those thoughts with others in a safe environment.

> • Explain to the group that you want them to think back over their experiences of management support and make a brief note on a 'Post-It' of what they found helpful or unhelpful. Encourage them to offer comments on both the positive and negative aspects. When they all have something to contribute, ask them to post the 'what I found helpful' comments on the designated wall space or board and the 'what I found unhelpful' ones in a different designated place (about 15 minutes

should be sufficient, but allow time for everyone to think of at least one positive and one negative experience).

• Once they have all been posted, allow the group time to wander around and look at the comments that have been displayed (10 minutes).

• Now reconvene as a main group and invite discussion about how they feel after reading each other's comments - whether they have noticed any themes, and so on (about 10 minutes). When they have had the chance to air any general comments, explain that you want them to go into pairs to reflect on this final question:

> – Your manager has responsibilities in terms of staff care, but what part can **you** play in ensuring that you get the support and feedback that will help you to work to the best of your abilities?

• This should take another 10 to 15 minutes. Finally, spend 10 minutes or so bringing the exercise to an end by drawing out any tips or strategies that people are willing to share with the rest of the group, supplementing these with your own suggestions if necessary. This will help to ensure that the day ends on a positive and hopeful note.

Suggested Further Reading

Cottrell, S. (2005) *Critical Thinking Skills: Developing Effective Analysis and Argument*, Basingstoke, Palgrave Macmillan.

Clutterbuck, D. (1998) *Learning Alliances: Tapping into Talent*, London, Chartered Institute of Personnel and Development.

Ghaye, T. and Lillyman, S. (2006) *Learning Journals and Critical Incidents: Reflective Practice for Health Care Professionals*, 2nd edn, London, Quay Books.

Morrison, T. (2001) *Supervision in Social Care*, 2nd edn, Brighton, Pavilion.

SCIE (2004) *Learning Organisations: A Self-Assessment Resource Pack*, London, SCIE.

Shohet, R. (ed.) (2007) *Passionate Supervision*, London, Jessica Kingsley.

Pritchard, J. (1994) *Good Practice in Supervision: Statutory and Voluntary Organisations*, London, Jessica Kingsley.

Thompson, N. (2006) *Promoting Workplace Learning*, Bristol, The Policy Press.

Thompson, S. and Thompson, N. (2008) *The Critically Reflective Practitioner*, Basingstoke, Palgrave Macmillan.

Waldman, J. (1999) *Help Yourself to Learning at Work*, Lyme Regis, Russell House Publishing.

Training Exercises: Discrimination and Oppression

Introduction to Part Two

Part Two comprises a separate collection of exercises that focus more specifically on discrimination and oppression than some of the preceding ones. We have chosen to structure the manual in this way in order to reflect the high profile that these issues attract in the three books with which this manual is linked. Of course, this is not to say that anti-discriminatory values and practice are unimportant with regard to those issues that feature in Part One – far from it – but it will provide food for thought where you want participants to explore discrimination and oppression in particular.

Power and Empowerment

Setting the Scene

Power is a complex phenomenon which incorporates many different aspects and, as such, is very difficult to pin down with a precise definition. This is because it operates in many different ways and at many different levels. We do not have the space here to explore the complexities of this important concept and so would urge you to read what people have to say about it if you are not already familiar with the subject – Neil Thompson's book, *Power and Empowerment*, in the *Theory into Practice* series (see the suggestions for further reading at the end of this section), is a short and accessible introductory text, which highlights the need to engage with issues of power because of its importance for all forms of people work.

In the context of working with adults we have included a section on power and empowerment because, where there are people and where there are finite resources, there will always be relationships of power whereby some groups in society lose out to others. This could be in an economic sense, but also in terms of being considered 'less than' other sectors – for example, where older people are seen as a burden, or services are designed from ethnocentric perspectives which do not recognise the unique needs of individuals from ethnic groups other than their own.

When working with adults we are often helping to address vulnerability and, while that vulnerability manifests itself in individuals, it is not necessarily the individual's fault. For example, power can be seen to be operating where it helps in the creation of vulnerability and dependency, such as when housing estates are built without shops and pharmacies so that people are forced to travel to do essential shopping; when public transport budgets do not allocate enough resources for disabled people who then have to use expensive private transport; when services focus heavily on providing care for dependent adults at the expense of rehabilitative and enabling initiatives; and so on.

The exercises which follow are designed to get power and empowerment (which tend to operate unseen) out in the open and on the agenda for discussion. Because of their importance, power and empowerment are key themes in all three of the *Theory into Practice* books, but we would draw attention to the following in particular:

Safeguarding Adults: The discussions about vulnerability and abuse in Chapters 1 and 2 provide useful background material to inform discussions about power, as do Chapters 5 and 6, which focus on service user involvement and discrimination and oppression in general.

Community Care: Chapter 6 has a specific focus on empowerment, but relevant material can also be found in Chapter 3 on empowerment and Chapter 10 with its focus on equality assurance.

Age Discrimination: As the title suggests, the whole book is relevant here, in that it has an emphasis on discrimination against older people and the oppression that results from the abuse of power. Part Two contains short sections on vulnerability and service user involvement.

Exercise 8.1.

Power - Exploring the Concept

Aim

This is designed to facilitate an exploration of power as a concept.

Materials

A sheet of flip chart paper and a marker pen for each group; white board or flip chart for presentation and recording feedback.

Timing

Allow an hour to 75 minutes for this exercise.

Notes for trainer

For a more in-depth account of aspects of power see Chapter 1 of Thompson (2007).

Activity

• Discussion in small groups followed by a sharing of ideas.

• Begin by offering a short presentation (about 10 to 15 minutes) about the four aspects of power highlighted as follows by Neil Thompson in his book *Power and Empowerment* (2007):

    – Power to: in the sense of using one's power to help people achieve their potential.
    – Power over: this refers to unequal power relations and can refer to both legitimate authority and to the abuse of power which results in oppression.
    – Power with: referring to the benefits to be gained from working together, rather than alone or against another person or organisation.
    – Power from within: using our own inner strengths and resilience to achieve successes and helping others to draw on theirs.

• Then ask the group to break off into small groups or pairs and discuss how what has been presented relates to their practice. For each of the four aspects they should try to think of examples where power has, or could have been, used in these ways (allow about 30 to 40 minutes).

• With the groups back together as one main group, invite feedback and draw out any themes, tips and learning points that have arisen from the exercise (15 to 20 minutes).

Control, Influence, Accept

Aim

This is designed to make the point that power is not a constant – that is, it is not the case that we are either powerful or powerless. We can exercise power and feel differently in different circumstances.

Materials

A sheet of flip chart paper and marker for each group – the sheet (held horizontally in landscape format), needs to have been pre-marked into three equal divisions, the first column headed C, the middle one I and the third one A; white board or flip chart for recording feedback.

Timing

Allow about an hour for this exercise.

Activity

• This is suitable for small group work, but can also be used by individuals as an aid to learning.

• Begin this exercise by explaining what the letters C, I and A represent – that is, control/influence/accept. Spend a few minutes with the group exploring the notion that, in terms of power, there will some things that they have the power to control or change (direct power), others where they have no ultimate control but they can influence those who do hold the power (indirect power), and other situations where they have no power to promote change and so have to accept or work around a situation (5 to 10 minutes).

• Then ask the group to break off into pairs or small groups and use the pre-marked flip chart sheets to record how they feel these aspects of power relate to their own practice (30 to 40 minutes).

• With the main group back together, draw out the key learning points that have arisen in terms of furthering the participants' understanding of the power issues connected with their practice (10 to 15 minutes).

Exercise 8.3.

Are Some More Powerful than Others?

Aim

The user involvement movement in general has, in recent decades, made major strides towards ensuring that those who work with adults in the human services do so in a spirit of partnership with those they provide a service for. There is now more of an expectation that decisions be made with, rather than on behalf of service users, unless their capacity to do so is impaired to the extent that they cannot make informed choices. In this exercise participants are encouraged to explore the concept of user and carer involvement and consider to what extent power is really 'shared'.

Materials

Copies of the worksheet - Are Some More Powerful than Others?; white board or flip chart for recording feedback.

Timing

Allow 50 minutes to an hour for this exercise.

Notes for trainer

The questions on this worksheet reflect the situation of staff working in residential settings. If you wish to use it with groups other than residential care workers, you will need to substitute questions that relate to the specific needs.

Activity

• As it involves worksheets, this is suitable for small group work but can be used by individuals as an aid to study.

• You will need to begin with a short presentation (approximately 10 minutes) about the four terms of reference that Hickey (1994) uses when analysing service user involvement. In his research, he was comparing two organisations to assess whether the democratisation of services had benefited those who used them. We would suggest that his breakdown of the levels at which 'supposed' partnership in decision making provides a very useful one for helping participants to explore power sharing in their own practice. His distinctions are paraphrased as follows:

- Explanation to service users of decisions already taken
- Consultation with service users prior to decisions being taken on their behalf
- Partnership with service users in decision-making processes
- User control of decision-making processes

• After discussing these elements with the participants, ask them to break off into pairs or small groups and work through the worksheet. Explain that, for each of the questions, they will need to identify where, in their own establishment and opinion, the power to decide lies (that is, to what extent do service users have a say). We would suggest allowing about 20 minutes for this part of the exercise.

• Ask the groups to reconvene as a main group and then take feedback about what they have learned about power and power sharing from this activity (10 to 15 minutes).

Are Some More Powerful than Others?

In the context of your own workplace, consider at what level the residents you work with have any control of, or input into, decisions about lifestyle choices.

- Level 1 - Explanation of decisions already taken
- Level 2 - Consultation prior to decision making you do on their behalf
- Level 3 - Partnership in decision-making processes
- Level 4 - User control in decision-making processes

When you have done so, think about what your answers say about the power balance between givers and receivers of care and about the valuing or otherwise of partnership and rights.

Getting up and going to bed: Level 1 ☐ Level 2 ☐ Level 3 ☐ Level 4 ☐

How to spend leisure time: Level 1 ☐ Level 2 ☐ Level 3 ☐ Level 4 ☐

Where to receive visitors: Level 1 ☐ Level 2 ☐ Level 3 ☐ Level 4 ☐

Whether to own a pet: Level 1 ☐ Level 2 ☐ Level 3 ☐ Level 4 ☐

When and whether to eat: Level 1 ☐ Level 2 ☐ Level 3 ☐ Level 4 ☐

Treatment regimes: Level 1 ☐ Level 2 ☐ Level 3 ☐ Level 4 ☐

Risk taking: Level 1 ☐ Level 2 ☐ Level 3 ☐ Level 4 ☐

Promoting Interdependency

Aim

Vulnerable adults are often seen as one-dimensional, that is as dependent. However, few are dependent in every respect. In this exercise we explore how this stereotype of vulnerable adults as dependent can be challenged by the promotion of opportunities for reciprocity – the 'giving back' that can challenge power relationships based on dependency and promote interdependency instead.

Materials

A sheet of flip chart paper and marker pen for each group; Blutack or similar for displaying the sheets on a wall (if allowed); white board or flip chart for recording feedback.

Timing

Allow about an hour for this exercise.

Activity

• As it is about reflection, this exercise can be used with one main group, a set of small groups, or for individual study.

• Ask the group to break off into pairs or form small groups. Give each a sheet of paper and a marker to record ways in which they feel able to 'give back' to the people in their lives – what it is that makes them feel useful or good about themselves and contributes to their self-esteem. When they have had time (about 15 to 20 minutes) to do so, ask all of the groups to display their flip chart sheets on a wall or table and allow 5 to 10 minutes for participants to read each others' contributions.

• With the group back as a whole ask them to consider:

1. Whether the adults they work with have similar opportunity to 'give back' and build their self-esteem as valuable citizens – to contribute in ways not compromised by the factor or factors that have led to them being labelled as dependent, and
2. Where it exists, how that imbalance of power could be challenged.

• When the group have had chance to feed back their thoughts on the above (allow about 20 minutes) spend a final few minutes drawing out the key learning points that have arisen in terms of the group's understanding of power and power sharing.

Suggested Further Reading

Adams, R. (2003) *Social Work and Empowerment*, 3rd edn, Basingstoke, Palgrave Macmillan.

Clark, J. (2006) *Just Ordinary People: William Francis Blunn 'Our Bill'*, Liverpool, Moving on with Life and Learning.

Hugman, R. (1991) *Power in Caring Professions*, Basingstoke, Macmillan – now Palgrave Macmillan.

Humphries, B. (ed.) (1996) *Critical Perspectives on Empowerment*, Birmingham, Venture Press.

Jack, R. (ed.) (1995) *Empowerment in Community Care*, London, Chapman and Hall.

Thompson, N. (2003) *Promoting Equality: Challenging Discrimination and Oppression*, 2nd edn, Basingstoke, Palgrave Macmillan.

Thompson, N. (2007) *Power and Empowerment*, Lyme Regis, Russell House Publishing.

Thursz, D., Nusberg, C. and Prather, J. (eds) (1995) *Empowering Older People: An International Approach*, London, Cassell.

Discrimination

Setting the scene

We have included a section on discrimination because of the potential for some service users to be disadvantaged and, indeed, harmed as a consequence of being conceptualised as not only different, but also less deserving of respect and resources than others. The word 'discriminate' literally means to differentiate, but it has come to incorporate a sense of discrimination *against*, so that, as Thompson (2003) explains, ' ...negative discrimination involves not only identifying differences but also making a negative attribution – attaching a negative or detrimental label or connotation to the person, group or entity concerned' (p.10). Where these negative connotations are allowed to flourish they become accepted as a justification for treating people less favourably, purely on the basis of assumed inferiority, be it on the grounds of class, gender, race, ethnicity, ability, religion, sexual orientation or whatever. The abuse of power which results from discrimination operates in many different ways (for example, by marginalising certain groups and trivialising their contribution to society) and at different levels. For example, discrimination can be seen to operate at the level of individual prejudices and actions (such as ridicule) but is also reinforced at a cultural level where it is seen as acceptable to, for example, laugh at old people and exclude disabled people from mainstream activities because of poor or non-existent access to buildings and transport systems. Furthermore, it operates at a broader level again, where the unequal power relations which sustain 'the status quo' remain unchallenged or only marginally addressed by structural factors in society, such as the political system.

Discrimination is not always overt or intentional, but the consequences are unfair and harmful nevertheless. The selection of exercises which follows cannot do justice to such an important and broad-ranging issue as discrimination, but will help participants to begin to analyse whether there is a discriminatory element to the work they undertake with adults, be it in their own practice or as a representative of a wider organisation, service or system. Given that those working in the field are generally caring people, it is unlikely to be intentional but, where it can be recognised, it can be addressed – that is, where we are not challenging discrimination, we are reinforcing it.

Community Care: because of the underpinning themes of empowerment and partnership, we would suggest that the whole book has an emphasis on anti-discriminatory practice. However, Chapters 6 and 10 have particular relevance.

Safeguarding Adults: as the book talks about power and abuse of power then all of it is relevant but there is aparticular focus in Chapter 6.

Age Discrimination: as the title suggests, the whole book is about a particular form of discrimination – on the grounds of age, but the general discussion is transferable.

Discrimination - Exploring the Concept (i)

Aim

This exercise is designed to help test out and further people's understanding of the concept and to highlight diversity and difference as something to be valued and promoted, rather than being seen as problematic and negative.

Materials

White board or flip chart for recording feedback.

Timing

Allow about 30 minutes for this exercise.

Notes for trainer

The exercises in this section are premised on the trainer having a good understanding of this complex and important field. You may want to consider bringing in another trainer if you do not feel comfortable with the material or with handling the discussions that will arise from it.

Activity

• This exercise is a 'brainstorming' activity designed to be used with a group.

• With the group all together, write the word 'discrimination' in the centre of the white board or flip chart where everyone can see it. Ask the participants to tell you what the word conjures up for them. As you write these responses on the white board or flip chart, link them with a line to the original word in the centre. When you feel that there is enough on the diagram to highlight the complexity of the term, ask them to tell you whether they can see any links or themes from what has been produced this far (about 15 minutes).

• Draw the exercise to a close by asking the group what this tells us about discrimination. If comments about how commonly it occurs, how complex a concept it is, and how it inter-relates with other processes do not arise spontaneously, you will need to flag them up, as this has been the purpose of the process (about 15 minutes). In the summing up, it is important to revisit the point made in the section on 'aim' about promoting diversity as something to be valued, rather than seeing difference as a basis for discrimination.

Discrimination - Exploring the Concept (ii)

Aim

This exercise is useful for broadening and deepening participants' understanding of key terms associated with discrimination.

Timing

This will be variable depending on the size of the group and the number of cards you have available for use because both will affect how many combinations there are for discussions with partners. You may want to put a time limit on this exercise, especially if the group is a large one.

Notes for trainer

In preparation for this exercise you will need to make up cards on which you have written important terms or concepts to do with discrimination. Some examples and brief notes have been included (for your eyes only). Add to them or design others if you wish or, if all the participants work in the same field, you might want to adapt them to reflect the experiences of a particular user group. As with all of the exercises connected with this complex and sensitive field, we would suggest that you use them only if you feel confident about your understanding of the material and the discussions that may arise.

Activity

• This involves a group of people moving around the room to speak to different people, and then reconvening as one group to report back on what they have learned from this process.

• After explaining the exercise and its purpose, issue each person with a card and ask them to spend a few minutes in private thought about what they understand the term on their card to mean. If you feel that some of the participants are unconfident, you could begin the exercise with pairs rather than individuals. Then, explain that they need to get up and move around the room, seeking out someone they haven't spoken to before, and comparing notes about what they understand by the terms on each others' cards. Once they have had feedback from that person, they need to approach a different person and get more feedback in the same way. When they have had the opportunity to get feedback from several other people (if it is a large group there may not be time to speak to everyone), reconvene the main group and ask each person (or pair) in turn to:

1. Let the rest of the group know what the term on their card is;
2. Explain what they understand by it; and
3. Say how talking to others has furthered their understanding of it in any way.

• Spend the last few minutes drawing out any learning issues that have arisen from this exercise and flagging them up for further attention if necessary.

Discrimination – used in this sense to refer to negative or unfair discrimination, whereby people or groups are not only identified as different, but have a negative connotation attached to that difference.

Oppression – described by Thompson (2006b) as 'Inhuman or degrading treatment of individuals or groups; hardships and injustice brought about by the dominance of one group over another; the negative and demeaning exercise of power' [p. 40].

Diversity – refers to social variety. The diversity approach promotes the valuing of difference as something to be celebrated rather than it being seen as a problem.

Ethnocentrism – the tendency to see situations from one's own cultural perspective and in the context of the values and expectations associated with that culture. Ethnicity is often understood as something that people outside of our own culture have and which marks them out as different, but ethnicity is a dimension we all have. To refer to someone as 'ethnic' is therefore meaningless and potentially derogatory because it marks them out as different from what is perceived to be 'the norm'.

Institutional oppression – this refers to the point that oppression does not only result from the actions and attitudes of individuals but can be built into, for example, organisational policies, such as working hours which make life unnecessarily difficult for those with additional caring responsibilities (typically women).

Ageism – This is the process, or set of processes, whereby people are discriminated against purely on the grounds of their age, even though there is not necessarily a correlation between age and competence. It is most often used to refer to discrimination against older people but includes that against younger people too – you may want to include sexism, racism, heterosexism and disablism as examples of other discriminatory processes.

Stereotype – When this term is used, it tends to reflect the negative aspect of stereotyping. In order to manage information, we all tend to group people and things together as a form of shorthand – for example, women, men, ethnic minority populations, people of a particular sexual orientation and so on. Stereotyping occurs when particular (and usually negative) characteristics are attributed to such groups or classifications, and where they are perpetuated even when there is evidence to contradict those assumptions. So, for example, an enduring stereotype of Irish people is that they are stupid, even though there are many, many intelligent and educated Irish people.

Institutional Discrimination

Aim

We have included this exercise to ensure that there is a specific focus on institutional discrimination and the role that it plays in perpetuating discriminatory ideas, policies and practices.

Materials

Copies of the worksheet - Institutional Discrimination; white board or flip chart for recording feedback.

Timing

Allow about an hour to 75 minutes.

Activity

> • This involves using case scenarios to generate discussion and so is suited to small group work. It can also be used as an aid to individual study.

> • With the participants together as a main group, make a short presentation about institutional discrimination so that you are sure that everyone understands the basic concept (about 10 minutes should suffice). Then ask the participants to break off into pairs or small groups and help each other to explore the scenarios on the worksheet. We would suggest about 10 minutes per scenario.

> • With the main group reconvened spend about 15 minutes or so drawing out the learning points that have arisen.

Institutional Discrimination

Study A

One afternoon at work, Jim, the assistant manager of a nursing home for older people, was taken ill with stomach pains and admitted to hospital, where he was admitted to a ward and seen by a doctor who specialised in gastro-intestinal problems. Ken, one of the residents, had also had stomach pains a few weeks earlier and he too had been admitted to hospital, but under the care of a geriatrician.

What does this tell us about how older people are conceptualised in society?

Can discrimination at this level be easily addressed?

What does this tell us about institutional discrimination?

Study B

Andy had been a volunteer for over a year at a drop in centre for people with drug-related problems and was keen to enrol on a social care course so that he could embark on a career in this field. However, because of his particular disability, there were no facilities at the college that would allow him to communicate and submit written work within a timescale he could manage and he knew that he would not be able to work fast enough to keep to the programme's schedule for assignment submissions.

What does this tell us about how disabled people are conceptualised in society?

Can discrimination at this level be easily addressed?

What does this tell us about institutional discrimination?

Study C

Samantha had launched her private care agency almost a year ago. She had underestimated how much it would cost to get her business up and running and so, in order to save on advertising costs, she had asked her core group of six full-time staff to let people in their own families and social network know that she wanted to recruit carers. This had worked in terms of numbers, as she now had more than 30 carers on her books. But, all were white and female. She didn't think this mattered because to her, 'caring is the same the world over'.

What does this tell us about how people from ethnic minorities are conceptualised in society?

Can discrimination at this level be easily addressed?

What does this tell us about institutional discrimination?

Study D

Hal and John had come to the conclusion that they could no longer manage to live together in the home that they had shared for 25 years and decided to move together to a residential home where they could receive the support they wanted. They wanted to ensure that the home's ethos matched with their own outlook on life but, even though money was no object to them, they were unable to find any within travelling distance of their friends and family that offered provision for same-sex couples.

What does this tell us about how gay people are conceptualised in society?

Can discrimination at this level be easily addressed?

What does this tell us about institutional discrimination?

Challenging Discrimination

Aim

This draws on the learning from the previous exercises and facilitates reflection about the implications of this learning for the participants' own practice.

Materials

White board or flip chart for recording feedback; If dividing the group into smaller ones, a sheet of flip chart paper and marker pen for each group.

Timing

Allow about an hour for this exercise.

Notes for trainer

During the feedback, participants may need reminding that, when considering what they can do to challenge discrimination, this does not have to be direct action - they can play a role in influencing others.

Activity

• This is about reflection and the sharing of ideas. Dividing the main group into smaller groups is likely to stimulate these processes, but it can be used with one larger group if preferred.

• Remind the participants of the key issues they have covered this far (5 to 10 minutes). Then ask them to consider the following questions:

– What steps are needed in order to make a challenge to situations in the broad field of human services work with adults where some people or groups are treated less favourably than others? (allow about 15 minutes)

– In your own area of practice, what can you do to challenge discrimination? (about 15 minutes).

• Finally, spend a further 15 to 20 minutes or so drawing out the key learning points that have arisen from the exercise.

Suggested Further Reading

Baxter, C. (ed.) (2003) *Managing Diversity and Inequality in Healthcare*, London, Baillière Tindall.

Evans, R. and Banton, M. (2001) *Learning From Experience: Involving Black Disabled People in Shaping Services*, Warwickshire, Council of Disabled People.

Moss, B. (2007) *Values,* Lyme Regis, Russell House Publishing.

Pilkington, A. (2003) *Racial Disadvantage and Ethnic Diversity in Britain*, Basingstoke, Palgrave Macmillan.

Saraga, E. (ed.) (1998) *Embodying the Social: Constructions of Difference*, London, Routledge.

Thompson, N. (2003) *Promoting Equality: Challenging Discrimination and Oppression,* 2nd edn, Basingstoke, Palgrave Macmillan.

Thompson, N. (2006) *Anti-Discriminatory Practice*, 4th edn, Basingstoke, Palgrave Macmillan.

Thompson, S. (2006) *Age Discrimination,* Lyme Regis, Russell House Publishing.

Vulnerability

Setting the scene

A vulnerable adult is defined in *No Secrets* (DOH, 2000) as someone:

> who is or who may be in need of community care services by reason of mental or other disability, age or illness; and who is or may be unable to take care of him or herself, or unable to protect him or herself against harm or exploitation. (section 2.3).

This definition is updated in the Safeguarding Adults guidance (ADDS, 2005) to:

> every adult "who is or may be eligible for community care services" facing a risk to their independence due to abuse or neglect. (1.14)

These definitions have been critiqued in *Safeguarding Adults* as placing the vulnerability with the person. If the vulnerability is in some way a part of the person or is a result of their level of ability or age, then this has two implications. Firstly, the person is in some way responsible for their vulnerability and secondly other people or systems are not responsible for it. *Safeguarding Adults* makes the point that it is society and other people that create vulnerability through social processes and individual actions.

Vulnerability is discussed in *Safeguarding Adults* and *Age Discrimination*. This section will explore the meaning of 'vulnerability' as well as look at responsibilities of human services workers to report any concerns about safeguarding adults issues.

Introductory Exercise

Aim

This activity is designed to help participants to explore what vulnerability means.

Materials

Paper and pens; white board or flip chart for recording feedback.

Timing

Allow about 30 minutes for this exercise.

Activity

> • Individual and small group discussion.
>
> • Ask participants to think of either a novel they have read or a television programme they have watched which is about a character or characters that are vulnerable. If you are asked what you mean by 'vulnerable', resist the temptation to define it, as part of the purpose of the exercise is to encourage a discussion about this and see what definitions participants already attach to the word. Ask participants to share their ideas while you write up the ideas on a flip chart pad.
>
> • Ask each participant to state why they thought the person or people were vulnerable. Once the list is complete ask participants to work in pairs to try and agree a definition of what it means to be vulnerable. Ask the pairs to share their definitions with the whole group. Ask participants to remember their definition as you will return to it later in the day to see if any changes are needed to it or not. Allow about 10 minutes for working on the definition.

Exercise 10.1.

The Social Model of Disability

Aim

In this exercise you will be looking at the social model of disability, as this underpins the critique of the legal definition that you will explore in the next exercise. The social model of disability is discussed in *Safeguarding Adults* and *Age Discrimination*. *Safeguarding Adults* summarises the social model of disability:

> The social model of disability states that some people do have mental or physical impairments, but it is not these that limit and restrict their inclusion in society. It is not the fact that a person uses a wheelchair to mobilise that means they cannot access some buildings. It is the fact that society constructs buildings which are known to be non-accessible to some members of that society. (p. 15)

The implication of the social model of disability is that it is people in society and society itself through social processes which disable a person, not any physical or mental condition or impairment that they may have. Explain this model to the group and ask for any comments on it. The response you have to it may well depend on what exposure participants have had to this idea before. If it is totally new to people, then it may be difficult for them to grasp as it goes against the medical model of disability which is widely held to be true in western society, although this is beginning to change as the medical model has been widely criticised.

Materials

Copies of Case Study 8; paper and pens, white board or flip chart for recording feedback.

Timing

Allow about 40 minutes for this exercise.

Activity

- For working in small groups.

- Ask the participants to read Case Study 8 and answer the questions that follow it in groups of 4 or 5. Allow 20 minutes for this discussion.

- Ask the groups to feed back on their discussion. Ask a different group to start the feedback on each question to ensure all groups have a chance to contribute.

- Overleaf is listed some thoughts on the three questions so that you can comment on the feedback or guide the discussion towards looking at the scenario from a social model perspective.

• Question 1 – the point here is that it is Mitzi's family that have disabled her, not her learning disability. There may be discussion about the level of Mitzi's learning disability or her ability to perform the tasks. However, although Mitzi may be able to learn tasks more quickly depending on her level of learning disability, the relevant point here is that it is not her ability or perceived lack of ability which explains her lack of domestic skills, but her lack of opportunity to develop any.

• Question 2 – Mitzi could have been supported to learn skills the same as any other person. She may have taken longer to learn them, or she may not. Children often learn by being allowed to help out and to take responsibility for a small part of a task or they may watch their parents or carers. Often disabled children don't have this opportunity because there are concerns about them hurting themselves or they are not expected to need the skills.

• Question 3 – now that Mitzi has reached early adulthood and has not learnt the skills which many children and young people learn as a matter of course, she will have to start to learn from the beginning. This is not the main barrier to her though. The main barrier is the fact that she has internalised the message that she is unable to do household chores and to gain key skills for being an independent adult. It is this psychological barrier which has to be overcome for her to succeed in living independently. This is not to say that Mitzi would still not have needed any support if she had learned skills at home as she may well have needed this. Living independently does not always mean doing everything yourself, but can mean living in your own flat or house with appropriate support.

Vulnerability

Aim

This exercise continues to explore what vulnerability is. It builds on the social model of disability to encourage discussion about a social model of vulnerability.

Materials

Copies of Case Study 9; paper and pens; white board or flip chart for recording feedback.

Timing

Allow about 40 minutes for this exercise.

Activity

- Work in small groups.

- In the previous exercise you have explored how people are disabled by other people, rather than by any impairment they might have.

- Ask them to work in the same groups as before and to read Case Study 9 and answer the accompanying questions. Allow 20 minutes for the discussion.

- Take feedback from the groups and again use the pointers below on the questions to support and comment on the feedback.

- Question 1 – you may have some people who think it was Mr Patel's depression due to his bereavement that made him vulnerable. However, if Mr Patel had been supported and listened to, then the situation could have unfolded very differently.

- Question 2 – there are a number of things that should have been done differently in the residential home, including a proper induction for the keyworker, a better system of communication between staff and the manager and training for staff on supporting people who have been bereaved and who are depressed.

- Question 3 – Mr Patel could have been supported differently by being offered counselling or someone to talk to about his bereavement. The GP should have been alerted much earlier and if Mr Patel still stayed in bed for long periods, then staff should have taken preventative measures to ensure he did not have pressure sores developing.

• Participants may well think of additional points to those outlined. The important message to be gained from this exercise is that it is the lack of appropriate support that made Mr Patel vulnerable. He could have coped far better with the appropriate support. The residential home was negligent in their care of Mr Patel at a time when he needed sensitive care and support.

Exercise 10.3.

Concerns and Responsibilities

Aim

This exercise will examine the responsibilities that human services workers have to report issues of concern about safeguarding adults.

Materials

A sheet of flip chart paper and pen for each group; white board or flip chart for recording feedback.

Timing

Allow about 45 minutes for this exercise.

Notes for trainer

You should be aware that any sessions that discuss abuse of any kind can raise powerful memories and feelings for some people. It is good practice to state at the beginning of this exercise that if anyone is upset and needs to take a break or go for some fresh air, then they may do so. It is also good practice to have information about local support and counselling services for abuse survivors that you should make available for anyone who may need them.

Activity

- Discussion in small groups.

- *Safeguarding Adults* states:

> It is not the role of any worker in day services, housing, a residential setting or any other setting where services are provided, to make a judgment about what is being alleged, nor to investigate the allegations, but to pass the concern on to the appropriate person. (p. 32)

- You may want to link this exercise with the safeguarding procedures in your own agency.

- Start the exercise by asking participants to tell you what kinds of abuse of adults there are. Write their responses on a white board or flip chart, so that all participants can see the list. The types of abuse are discussed in *Safeguarding Adults*. The types of abuse as detailed in *No Secrets* are:

  – Physical abuse
  – Sexual abuse

    – Psychological abuse
    – Financial or material abuse
    – Neglect or acts of omission
    – Discriminatory abuse

• Once you have all of the categories on your list, divide your participants into six groups if you have a large enough group, or three groups if not. Ask each group to take either one or two categories of abuse (depending on whether you have three or six groups). Ask each group to discuss how they might recognise that the adults they support have been subjected to the type(s) of abuse they are considering. Ask the groups to consider what they might hear, see or suspect. Allow 30 minutes for this discussion. Ask the groups to write up their discussion on flip chart paper.

• Take feedback from each group and ask other groups to contribute to the discussion about each category. The feedback should highlight signs that are visual, such as bruising, concerns that are heard, such as abuse being disclosed and concerns being raised by behaviour that is uncharacteristic in any way.

Exercise 10.4.

What Should I Do?

Aim

Following on from a consideration of the types of abuse, this exercise explores what a worker should do if they have reason to believe that an adult they are supporting is being abused or they are alerted to the possibility of abuse.

Materials

Copies of Case Study 10; white board or flip chart for recording feedback.

Timing

30 minutes or an hour if you go through your own agency procedures as well as the guidance detailed below.

Notes for trainer

The list below should either be pre-written on flip chart paper or put on an overhead transparency or given as a handout so participants can see it as you refer to it.

Activity

• This offers an opportunity to develop both understanding and skills in working with vulnerable people.

• *Safeguarding Adults* discusses what a worker should do if they are alerted to the possibility of abuse. It cites the list in ADSS (2005) which offers good practice advice for human services workers in such circumstances:

– Remaining calm and not showing shock or disbelief
– Listening carefully to what is being said
– Not asking detailed or probing questions
– Demonstrating a sympathetic approach by acknowledging regret and concern that what has been reported has happened
– Ensuring that any emergency action needed has been taken
– Confirming that the information will be taken seriously
– Giving them information about the steps that will be taken
– Informing them that they will receive feedback as to the result of the concerns they have raised and from whom
– Giving the person contact details so they can report any further issues or ask any questions that may arise (9.3.7)
(p 33)

126

• Go through this list with participants and discuss with the group why each of them is important.

• Ask the participants to read Case Study 10. When they have read it, ask them to work in pairs. Ask the pairs to take it in turns to be Ernest and the care worker and to act out the situation where Ernest reports his concerns about another resident. Ask that the participant that plays the role of the care worker takes account of the list reproduced overleaf in their responses to Ernest. Allow about 10 minutes for this activity.

• Once the pairs have had a chance to play both roles, ask the group to feed back how they found the exercise. Ask them if they are clear about how to support people who are disclosing about abuse and also if they are clear about who they should pass these concerns on to. At this point you may want to make sure that all participants are aware of your known agency procedures about alerting concerns of abuse to the statutory authority.

Suggested Further Reading

Brown, K. (2003) *Vulnerable Adults and Community Care: A Reader*, Exeter, Learning Matters.

Parker, J. and Penhale, B. (2007) *Working with Vulnerable Adults*, London, Routledge.

Pritchard, J. (2001) *Good Practice with Vulnerable Adults,* London, Jessica Kingsley.

Pritchard, J. (2007) *Working with Adult Abuse: A Training Manual For People who Work with Vulnerable People*, London, Jessica Kingsley.

Language Sensitivity

Setting the Scene

We have included a set of exercises on language sensitivity because of the potential that language has to either reinforce or challenge discrimination and oppression when working with adults who are experiencing difficulties. For example, language use can serve to include or exclude people or groups, imply a hierarchy of expertise or a commitment to valuing the contribution of others. It is unfortunate that the need to be sensitive to how words convey meaning has been trivialised by the 'political correctness' movement because it has resulted in a situation where many people avoid using 'banned' or 'inappropriate' terminology because they are directed to, rather than because they understand and respect the power of those words to have a negative impact on people's lives and to contribute to the perpetuation of oppressive attitudes, cultures and structures. We need to get past the fear of 'saying the wrong thing' and move towards a more analytical approach to the use of language if we are not to put the adults with whom we work at a disadvantage. If we consider, for example, the use of the word 'black', then there is a significant difference between its use in the term 'blackboard' and in the term 'black day'. In the former it is used as a neutral word to describe the colour of an item – there is no connotation of negativity or inferiority. In the latter, however, there is a connotation of negativity – an association between blackness and misfortune. In conjunction with other terms such as 'black mark',' black sheep' and 'blackspot' it can be seen to perpetuate the association between whiteness and positive traits and blackness and negative ones. We can see, then, that to always avoid the word 'black' in case it causes offence is to miss the point entirely, but to recognise how its use in some circumstances can be offensive, or add to the 'drip feed' of negative connotations, is to go some way towards understanding the subtlety of language use and the part it can play in how we support and advocate for others.

Language sensitivity is sometimes dismissed as pettiness, but the following exercises are designed to highlight the power of language to make a difference and to help persuade those working with adults of the need to think critically about the subject, rather than avoiding or dismissing it. Raising consciousness of, and encouraging an exploration of the power of language will provide a starting point of understanding from which participants may be able to influence others. Given that these exercises refer to the written and spoken word, they can be useful for exploring any aspect of work with adults because communication is always involved in some form. More specifically to the three books in the series, you might want to make links with the following discussions and topics:

Community Care: The partnership discussions in Chapter 8 involve 'speaking the same language' with both co-workers and service users and not using jargon to exclude non-professionals. See also the references to assessment and the need to take into account that such words are imbued with a particular meaning in professional settings which may not be understood by lay people.

Safeguarding Adults: Chapters 1 and 2 in particular, raise issues in terms of the values and messages attached to terms such as 'vulnerability', 'abuse' and 'significant harm', so that words can ascribe an inferior or superior status and affect how someone is conceptualised and treated. See also 'Adults in a Victimising Society' in Chapter 3.

Age Discrimination: The ageist processes discussed in the introductory chapter highlight the power of terminology to reinforce a message or set of values – particularly those of infantilisation, welfarisation, medicalisation and dehumanisation. See also the discussion in Part Two of language as a force for change.

Language - Subtle but Powerful (i)

Aim

This exercise can be a useful one to start off a day with because it explores language and communication in general, before moving on to link it with practice. Because we use language every day it is something we tend to take for granted and not give much thought to unless it presents us with a problem. As such, its subtleties and power usually go unnoticed except by those who take a special interest in language issues. We are not advocating that people need to become experts, but we are advocating that they need to develop a heightened sensitivity to the communication processes that are going on between providers and users of services and of their actual and potential effects. This exercise is designed to help participants start that process of consciousness raising.

Materials

White board or flip chart for recording feedback;extra flip chart sheets and pens if used as small group activity.

Timing

Allow about 45 minutes for this exercise.

Notes for trainer

This can be done as a brainstorming exercise, with a partner or in small groups. If you start it as a brainstorming exercise but realise that participants are finding it difficult to get into the issues or are unsure of themselves, you might find that having someone else to bounce ideas off stimulates their thinking and helps them to feel more confident about offering responses.

Activity

• This is a group exercise which is designed to help build on a general understanding of what language does, especially in terms of its power to promote or inhibit change.

• Explain to the group that you are going to look at language use in general, which could include written or spoken language, sign language, body language or whatever form of language is used to make a connection between people. Begin by flagging up on the white board or flip chart some of the reasons why we use language – we offer some suggestions overleaf. You may find that participants want to add others but we would advise you not to allow the list to become too long or it will tend make the next part of the exercise unworkable. Do ensure, however, that there are negative as well as positive aspects (10 to 15 minutes).

information gathering
instructing
demeaning
expressing emotion
comforting
challenging
praising
excluding
hurting
engaging with
refusing
demoralising

• Once you have compiled a list, ask the participants to offer examples from their own day-to-day lives for some or all of the uses identified and to explore how the use of particular terms or tones has made them feel. This exercise should work to highlight how diverse language is and also how much of an impact the particular choice of words, or manner of their delivery, can make.

Language - Subtle but Powerful (ii)

Aim

This exercise builds on the previous one to encourage participants to explore the part that language use plays in practice situations.

Materials

Paper and pens; white board or flip chart for recording feedback; access to the list of processes produced in Exercise 11.1 if you wish to use it.

Timing

Allow 40 minutes to an hour for this exercise.

Activity

- This exercise involves discussion in small groups.

- Ask the participants to work as partners or in small groups to share examples from their own practice (or that which they have witnessed) which highlight for them the effect that language use has had on situations in which they have been involved – particularly in terms of excluding people or making them feel inferior. In order to keep the discussions focused you might want to allocate each group an aspect or selection from those that were highlighted in Exercise 11.1

- Some groups might find it difficult to think of examples, and so it might be useful to think ahead and have a few suggestions from your own experience to 'throw into the pot' in order to stimulate discussion. For example, it may be that the use of jargon in a meeting has made a service user (or a worker) feel powerless or excluded. You might get or offer examples where the choice of a particular word can make a significant difference to the message conveyed, as in the use of the term 'drug abuse' (which has a value judgement attached to it) and drug use (which does not). We suggest you allow about 15 to 20 minutes for this stage.

- As a plenary exercise with the main group, ask for feedback from the small groups and use this to draw out that language can be a powerful force for promoting an inclusive society which values diversity but can also be used to inhibit change and exclude or discriminate. Remind the group that the main purpose of the exercise has been to highlight how subtle yet powerful language can be and yet how taken for granted it tends to be (20 to 30 minutes).

Underlying Messages

Aim

This exercise continues with the theme of the power of language to promote a particular message or ideology and therefore to reinforce or challenge the inequities which many adults face.

Materials

Copies of the worksheets - Underlying Messages and The Power of Language; white board or flip chart for plenary session.

Timing

Allow about an hour for this exercise.

Notes for trainer

There are two worksheets associated with this exercise. You may choose to use either or both, depending on the time available and the level of discussion that the exercises promote.

Activity

• The worksheets can be completed by individuals or collectively in small groups to provide the basis for a group discussion about the power of language to shape ideas and influence actions.

• Explain the purpose of the exercise and distribute copies of the worksheet to each participant. Even if working in small groups, they may still wish to complete their own copy (5 minutes).

• Allow 15 minutes or so for the participants to work though the first worksheet. If the groups can easily reconvene as a main group, then you may wish to take feedback at this point before asking them to go back into their smaller groups to complete the second worksheet. If you prefer to minimise disruption then ask for both worksheets to be completed before having a discussion as a main group about how language can shape our thinking in subtle ways if we are not sensitive to these processes. Whichever way you choose to organise this exercise, we would suggest allowing 15 minutes or so for each worksheet and a further 20 to 30 minutes or so for drawing out the learning points which arise from them.

Underlying Messages

What assumptions are the following sentences conveying?

She was quite intelligent for a woman.

....

All of the men responded so sensitively – it was amazing!

....

The instructions were written clearly and simply so that even old people would be able to follow them.

....

The invitation was extended to include the wives and dependants of senior managers.

....

We cater for all residents here. When there's a shopping trip on we always make sure that there's an alternative arranged for the men.

....

We don't have discos because we might get people with autism coming along and they don't like that sort of thing.

....

Delegates attending the conference on 'Social Attitudes to Disability' will be given assistance with registering and finding their seats in the main hall. All presenters should meet in Room 303, which can be reached by using the staircase at the back of the building.

....

There is no automatic door, but there is a voice-activated entry system located next to the keypad so disabled people will still have easy access. At the risk of sounding obvious, you just press the button and someone will answer and tell you what to do next.

....

Underlying Messages - Trainer's Guidance

What assumptions are the following sentences conveying?

She was quite intelligent for a woman

Women are not intelligent as a rule.

All of the men responded so sensitively – it was amazing!

Men are not sensitive as a rule, so this was something out of the ordinary.

The instructions were written clearly and simply so that even old people would be able to follow them.

People lose their intellectual abilities as they age, or only stupid people grow old.

The invitation was extended to include the wives and dependants of senior managers.

You have to be male to be a senior manager.

We cater for all residents here. When there's a shopping trip on we always make sure that there's an alternative arranged for the men.

No men like shopping. All women like shopping.

We don't have discos because we might get people with autism coming along and they don't like that sort of thing.

All people with autism are the same and autism affects them all in the same way.

Delegates attending the conference on 'Social Attitudes to Disability' will be given assistance with registering and finding their seats in the main hall. All presenters should meet in Room 303, which can be reached by using the staircase at the back of the building.

It implies that delegates are likely to be disabled and that they will need help with these tasks. It also implies that presenters are not likely to be disabled and won't have problems accessing the 3rd floor by staircase – links disability with dependency/passivity.

There is no automatic door but there is a voice-activated entry system located by the keypad so disabled people will still have easy access. At the risk of sounding obvious, you just press the button and someone will answer and tell you what to do next.

There is an assumption that everyone can speak, hear, read and comprehend.

The Power of Language

Why should the following terms be avoided? It is not sufficient to answer 'because we've been told not to'. The purpose of this exercise is to help you to think about how language has a great deal of power to affect how we think about things. That is, it can play a part in constructing the world in which we operate, as well as describing it.

Geriatric - *when used as a noun - that is, a geriatric.*

The elderly

A quadriplegic

Wheelchair bound

Ethnic (of a person or a community)

Career woman.

Where a person's disability is highlighted when it doesn't need to be – as in the example 'The Steering Committee meeting was chaired by blind key worker, Maggie Evans'.

The Power of Language - Trainer's Guidance

Why should the following terms be avoided? It is not sufficient to answer 'because we've been told not to'. The purpose of this exercise is to help you to think about how language has a great deal of power to affect how we think about things. That is, it can play a part in constructing the world in which we operate, as well as describing it.

Geriatric - when used as a noun - that is, a geriatric.

Geriatric is an adjective – that is, it describes someone as old and ill. Geriatrics is a medical speciality, as is paediatrics. While we never hear of a child being referred to as *a paediatric*, it is common for an older person to be described as *a geriatric*. The sense of that person as an individual is lost. The term is depersonalising and therefore it is demeaning.

The elderly

Again, this depersonalises – it denotes a mass group identity under which individual histories, unique personalities and so on are lost. It reinforces the view that all older people are the same – referring to the stereotype and not the individual.

A quadriplegic

Describes someone as a condition rather than a person. As such, it defines him or her by that condition, rather than portraying that person as an individual who has quadriplegia, but is more than the quadriplegia.

Wheelchair bound

This term is unduly negative. Many disabled people would say that their wheelchairs enable rather than bind them. This term reinforces the assumption that it is acceptable to describe a disabled person in terms of what he or she can't do or what is conceptualised as 'normal'.

Ethnic (of a person or a community)

'Ethnic' is often used to distinguish a person or community from one that is 'non-ethnic' as if ethnicity only refers to what a dominant culture sees as 'foreign'. In reality, we all have an ethnic dimension because it refers to what unites us as communities – for example a common language, religion, style of dress, set of customs and so on. To describe someone as 'ethnic' is therefore meaningless in one sense but derogatory in another because it gives out the message 'you are not like us'.

Career woman.

This terms helps to perpetuate the myth that woman's place is in the home and rearing children. The term 'career man' is not used because having a career is seen as being 'the norm' for a man, whereas for women it ought not to be assumed, according to the messages we receive as we are socialised into our culture.

Where a person's disability is highlighted when it doesn't need to be – as in the example 'The Steering Committee meeting was chaired by blind key worker, Maggie Evans'.

There are some instances where a person's disability needs to be highlighted but, in examples like this one, it only serves to mark out a person as different from what is considered to be the norm. If the person chairing the committee were not blind, would we see the report expressed as '… by sighted key worker, Maggie Evans?

Jargon - Who Benefits?

Aim

As with Exercise 11.3, this exercise highlights the power of language to exclude service users. Because most people working with adults in the broad field of human services will be caring people, it is unlikely that there will be deliberate intent on their part, but even where it is done inadvertently the outcome will be the same – that is, there will be an unequal relationship between those who receive and those who provide support and services. This exercise helps participants to appreciate other people's perspectives.

Materials

Paper and pens; white board or flip chart for recording feedback.

Timing

Allow about an hour for this exercise.

Activity

• This has been designed as a small group exercise, but both stages could also be carried out by individuals, or indeed as a main discussion group.

• You will need to begin the session with a brief exploration of what jargon means and a short discussion about its positive use – that is, how it can act as a shortcut to understanding and the sharing of knowledge and information when those concerned all know what a specific term means. At this point you could invite the participants to offer examples of where this happens in their own workplace. Then explain that you are going to move on to think about how using jargon can be unhelpful, rather than helpful (about 10 minutes).

– Then ask the participants to form small groups or partnerships and:

1. Think about situations in their daily lives where someone has used jargon (either intentionally or inadvertently) in conversation with them or in their presence.
2. Describe how that made them feel.

• Ask them to keep a record of the words and feelings that come out of the feedback from this exercise (or, if they are all in the same room and it is not too disruptive to take whole group feedback at this point, record them on a white board or flip chart at this point) - allow about 15 minutes.

• Next, ask the participants to remain in their groups but to now think about examples of the jargon that is used in their own workplaces (or where a commonly used word such as 'assessment' takes on a particular meaning in a specific context), and consider how someone not party to that shared understanding of terms might feel if it is used in their presence (perhaps in a multidisciplinary meeting or similar). When taking feedback from this stage of the exercise, try to write it on or near the feedback about their own experiences so that they can be compared (15 to 20 minutes).

• Finally, draw out the implications for practice, if partnership working is to be more than just tokenism (10 minutes).

Suggested Further Reading

Abley, M. (2003) *Spoken Here: Travels Among Threatened Languages*, London, William Heinemann.

Barker, C. and Galasinski, D. (2001) *Cultural Studies and Discourse Analysis: A Dialogue on Language and Identity*, London, Sage.

Hopkins, G. (1999) *Plain English for Social Services: A Guide to Better Communication,* Lyme Regis, Russell House Publishing.

Moss, B. (2008) *Communication Skills for Health and Social Care*, London, Sage.

Schirato, T. and Yell, S. (2000) *Communication and Culture: An Introduction*, London, Sage.

Thompson, N. (2003) *Communication and Language: A Handbook of Theory and Practice*, Basingstoke, Palgrave Macmillan.

Thompson, N. (2005) *Understanding Social Work* (Chapter 7), 2nd edn, Basingstoke, Palgrave Macmillan.

Workplace Culture

Setting the scene

Workplace culture is included in this training manual as it has a really important role to play in the actions of human services workers and how they work with the adults they support. Workplace culture is difficult to detect for those in the workplace as it is the 'way things are'. It is concerned with the attitudes of staff, the working practices that are adopted by staff, the language that people use about each other and the adults they support, the kind of humour that is prevalent and even the way staff dress. Workplace culture can have a really positive or negative effect on working practices and how service users are treated. If it is part of the workplace culture that service users are prioritised over the social needs of staff, then new members of staff will see this and be more likely to act accordingly. If, however, it is part of the workplace culture that service users are left to wait while staff chat and have long breaks, then this too is likely to shape the practice of new human services workers.

Workplace culture is discussed in *Safeguarding Adults*.

What is Culture?

Aim

This exercise is designed to help participants to explore the meaning of culture in general. It can be very difficult for people to understand the concept of culture, and so it might be appropriate to use the 'setting the scene' section at the beginning to form the basis of a short presentation to assist understanding if you feel this is necessary at this point.

Materials

Paper and pens; white board or flip chart for recording feedback.

Timing

Allow about 30 minutes for this exercise.

Activity

- For discussion in pairs.

- For this exercise, ask the participants to work in pairs. Ask them to write down what the word 'culture' means to them. Allow about 10 minutes for discussion and then ask for feedback. Write the responses on a white board or flip chart pad. Your responses may include food, language, religious observances, dress, and customs. Explain that it can be difficult to detect our own culture as we grow up in it and take it for granted. It is much easier to see other people's cultures, as the way they dress, the language they use, their customs and practices, such as the food they eat, are different from our own.

- Explain that families also have their own cultures within a culture. This can be evidenced by watching docudramas on the television which detail the lives of families. What is apparent by watching such programmes or by talking to other people about their family practices is how diverse they are. There are differences in ideas about child rearing, different practices in relation to gender roles, differences in how meals are prepared and eaten, whether as a family round a table or as individuals eating at separate times in front of the television on so on.

- If time allows, ask participants to work in pairs to discuss differences in their own family cultures around mealtimes, gender roles and holidays. Ask for feedback in the differences that participants found and the variety of family cultures that exist within your group.

Exercise 12.2.

Workplace Culture

Aim

This exercise moves the discussion on to the idea of workplace culture.

Materials

A sheet of flip chart paper and pen for each group; white board or flip chart for recording feedback.

Timing

Allow about 40 minutes for this exercise.

Activity

• Small group discussion.

• Explain that workplaces have their own cultures just as families do. Ask participants to work in groups of 4 or 5 to discuss what makes one workplace different from another. Ask the groups to think about working practices, language and customs when they are compiling their lists. It will help if participants have worked in more than one place, as this will help them think about how workplaces differ. You could give the groups an example to help them be clear about what you are asking them to do. One example is that in one residential home it is customary for staff members to have a chat after their handover between shifts so staff get to know one another, whereas in another residential home, once the handover has been completed, the staff who have just finished their shift go straight home and the other staff go and talk to the service users before starting their duties. Allow about 20 minutes for the discussion.

• You may need to go round to talk to each group to help them think of different aspects of workplaces, for example staff attitudes, humour, formality of relationships between staff and between staff and people they support.

• Give each group a piece of flip chart paper. Once the groups have discussed the task and recorded their thoughts ask each group to feed back to the whole group.

• When the groups have fed back, tell them that they have been identifying elements of workplace culture. These are often difficult to detect from within the workplace as they are 'how things are' in that working environment.

What is it Like Where You Work?

Aim

This exercise will help to further explore the culture in which participants work.

Materials

A pen and several pieces of 'Post-it' type sticky notes for each participant.

Timing

Allow about 30 minutes for this exercise.

Notes for trainer

For this exercise you should prepare three pieces of flip chart paper with the following headings written on the top:

- Humour
- Language
- Working practices

Put these pieces of flip chart paper up on the wall before the session starts.

Activity

- An interactive group activity.

- Ask the participants to imagine they are a new worker coming to join their place of work. As this new worker, ask them to imagine that they just observe all that happens in the workplace for the first week. Ask the participants to think about:

   – The kind of humour and jokes they would hear. What are the jokes about? Are they about service users or working situations?
   – The kind of language that is used about service users and about their lives.
   – What are the working practices? Are all working practices for the benefit of service users or not? Are all activities done for the benefit of service users? Who chooses the activities that service users engage in? Who chooses the meals that service users eat? Who chooses when people eat? If service users go away on holiday or out on trips, who chooses where these are? How is choice promoted in the workplace?

• Give participants some sticky labels and ask them to write their thoughts about what the new worker might see and hear and then stick them on the relevant flip chart paper that you have put up. Allow 15 minutes to complete this task.

• Ask the participants to look at the flip chart display once everyone has put their labels on.

• Once everyone has had a look at the display, ask if anyone has any comments on what they have seen. The discussion will be different, depending on whether your group is all from one work setting or from a number of settings. If participants are all from one work setting, then discussion should focus on whether there is agreement about what has been written and if not, why this might be. If the participants are from different work settings, then discussion can focus around how workplace cultures are different from each other. It would also be useful to note any similarities.

Workplace Culture - Helpful or Harmful?

Aim

This exercise will explore the idea of workplace culture as being helpful or harmful to service users.

Materials

Copies of Case Study 11; a sheet of flip chart paper and pen for each group; white board or flip chart for recording feedback.

Timing

Allow about 45 minutes for this exercise.

Activity

• Discussion in small groups with case study as a focus.

• Ask the participants to read Case Study 11 and to answer the questions set below it. Ask that participants work in small groups of about 4 or 5 and give them a piece of flip chart paper each to record their discussion. Allow about 30 minutes for this discussion.

• When the groups have finished their discussion ask them to feed back to the wider group. Below are some notes for you as pointers on what should be drawn out of the discussion:

• Question 1 – The Elms has a very positive culture for staff who work there, as they are friendly and supportive of each other. This makes a very pleasant working environment where staff feel they get a lot out of their job. However, the 'perks' are not for service users and instead are at their expense. A working culture like this may help with staff retention as it has a big social element to it and staff may not want to leave the friends that they work with.

• Question 2 – The Elms is unhelpful for service users. The service users may not actually be harmed physically, but they are not supported properly, as the time which should be spent with them is spend in staff socialising. They are also being discriminated against in that they are the victims of staff jokes, and although this may seem harmless, it is not. The attitude that underlies the humour of the jokes is one of the staff feeling that they are superior to the residents and it is all right to make fun of them. The culture is actually unhelpful for staff, as well as they are not developing professionally or getting the satisfaction they would from working in a more positive and enabling way with the people they support.

Exercise 12.4. cont.

• Question 3 – This is an interesting question, as rules and procedures can be put in place to address the issues, but these can still be worked around in a culture such as this one. The issue is about the attitudes of staff, and these can be passed on to new staff who want to fit in. The question is how to change attitudes and practices which result from these attitudes.

Positive Practices

Aim

This exercise follows on from question 3 of the previous exercise. The aims of this exercise are to reflect on the workplace culture and working practices in the place(s) where participants work and to promote working practices that do not disadvantage service users.

Materials

A sheet of flip chart paper and pen for each group; white board or flip chart for recording feedback.

Timing

Allow about 30 to 40 minutes for this exercise.

Activity

• Discussion in small groups.

• Ask the group to work in smaller groups of 3 or 4 people. Ask them to recall the work they did in Exercise 12.3 about their own workplace cultures. It is important that people work in small groups where the members are all from the same workplace. If this is not possible due to the composition of the group, then ask that participants who work in similar environments work together.

• Ask the groups to think about their own workplace culture and to make a list under the headings:

1. What is helpful to service users?
2. What is unhelpful to service users?

• Allow about 15 minutes to complete this task. Once the groups have completed the task, tell them that the first list should highlight areas of good practice whereas the second list should highlight areas which need to be addressed.

• Now ask the groups to address the items on their second list under the headings:

1. What can staff do differently to help address this issue?
2. How can we involve service users in addressing these issues?
3. How can we ensure that working practices are changed?

Summing up

How you sum up this session will depend on whether you are part of the workplace where participants work or not. If you are, then you can reach an agreement about how to implement the suggestions coming from the last exercise. If you are not, then you will need to ask the group how they want to take forward the suggestions from the last exercise.

It is important that these suggestions for how to work differently are not lost and also that the good practice which was highlighted is also acknowledged. Ask participants to agree a way of reviewing the progress of implementing the suggestions. Stress the importance of working with service users on this work. They may have a very different list of what should change if they were asked!

Suggested Further Reading

Banks, S. (2006) *Ethics and Values in Social Work*, 3rd edn, Basingstoke, Palgrave Macmillan.

Handy, C. (2005) *The New Completely Revised Understanding Organisations*, 3rd edn, London, Penguin Business.

Hofstede, G. and Hofstede, G.J. (2004) *Cultures and Organisations: Software for the Mind*, London, McGraw-Hill.

Thompson, N. (2003) *Promoting Equality, Challenging Discrimination and Oppression*, 2nd edn, Basingstoke, Palgrave Macmillan .

Thompson, N. (2006) *Anti-Discriminatory Practice,* 4th edn, Basingstoke, Palgrave Macmillan.

Conclusion

Our aim in this manual has been to help you to find ways of encouraging those practitioners who work with vulnerable and often dependent adults to critically evaluate the work that they do. We hope that the exercises and worksheets we have offered will provide opportunities to explore the extent to which their own practice, and the practices of their organisations, reflect a commitment to:

- working collaboratively with the users of the services they offer;
- the challenging of discrimination at all levels: and
- the valuing of service users' rights, including the right to take risks.

In designing these exercises we have tried to make them as user friendly as possible for the very broad range of fields that 'people work' covers. If some of them do not match your particular needs we hope that they will have inspired you to adapt or redesign them so that their message will reach your audience. If we have not included a topic or issue that you feel is an important one in terms of working with adults then it is because we have had to be selective for reasons of space. Adapt our exercises, or design your own so that you can enrich the learning experiences that will contribute to best practice with vulnerable, disempowered and marginalised adults.

References

Argyris, C. and Schön, D.A. (1974) *Theory in Practice: Increasing Personal Effectiveness*, San Francisco, Jossey-Bass.

Association of Directors of Social Services (ADSS) (2005) *Safeguarding Adults: A National Framework of Standards for Good Practice and Outcomes in Adult Protection Work*, London, ADSS.

Cooperrider, D., Whitney, D. and Stavros, J. (2003) *Appreciative Inquiry Handbook*, San Fransisco, Lakeshore Communications Inc. and Berrett-Koehler Publishers.

Doel, M. and Shardlow, S. M. (2005) *Modern Social Work Practice: Teaching and Learning in Practice Settings*, Aldershot, Ashgate.

Gray, C. (2002) *My Social Stories Book*, London, Jessica Kingsley.

Hickey, G. (1994) 'Towards a Responsive Service', *Community Care*, 26th May.

Jolles, R. (2005) *How to Run Seminars and Workshops: Presentation Skills for Consultants, Trainers and Teachers*, New Jersey, NJ, John Wiley and Sons.

Klatt, B. (1999) *The Ultimate Training Workshop Handbook*, Maidenhead, McGraw-Hill.

Koprowska, J. (2005) *Communication and Interpersonal Skills in Social Work*, Exeter, Learning Matters.

Martin, J. (2007) *Safeguarding Adults*, Lyme Regis, Russell House Publishing.

Redmond, B. (2006) *Reflection in Action Developing Reflective Practice in Health and Social Services,* Aldershot, Ashgate Publishing.

Smale, G. and Tuson, G. with Biehal, N. and Marsh, P. (1993) *Empowerment, Assessment, Care Management and the Skilled Worker*, London, HMSO.

Social Care Institute for Excellence (2006) *Adult Services Practice Guide 09: Dignity in Care*, London, SCIE.

Thompson, N. (2002) *People Skills*, 2nd edn, Basingstoke, Palgrave Macmillan.

Thompson, N. (2003) *Promoting Equality: Challenging Discrimination and Oppression*, 2nd edn, Basingstoke, Palgrave Macmillan.

Thompson, N. (2006a) *People Problems*, Basingstoke, Palgrave Macmillan.

Thompson, N. (2006b) *Anti-Discriminatory Practice*, 4th edn, Basingstoke, Palgrave Macmillan.

Thompson, N. (2007) *Power and Empowerment*, Lyme Regis, Russell House Publishing.

Thompson, N. and Thompson, S. (2005) *Community Care*, Lyme Regis, Russell House Publishing.

Thompson, S. (2005) *Age Discrimination*, Lyme Regis, Russell House Publishing.

Jake

Jake is 22 years old and has a condition which makes it extremely difficult for him to move or speak because of prolonged and painful muscle spasms. His intellectual capacities are unaffected. With help from his local authority he manages to live semi-independently in a purpose-built flat attached to his mother's house. Two carers visit several times each day to help him with getting in and out of bed, dressing and feeding, and he has a network of friends who visit him, usually unannounced, to chat and to help him with his home-based studying. One morning, only one of his carers turned up. She told Jake that she would do her best under the circumstances. With only one person to help him eat, most of his breakfast ended up on his pyjamas and bedclothes. The carer would not contravene health and safety guidelines by getting him out of bed on her own, and so she told Jake that he would have to spend the day in bed. His anxiety about this made his spasms worse so that he was unable to make her understand his request for that day's visit from his tutor to be cancelled. She told him she would leave a note pinned to the front door so that the other team of carers, due to visit mid-afternoon, would understand why he was still in bed when they called.

In what ways was Jake's dignity compromised here?

What avenues are open to Jake in terms of helping to ensure that his need for dignity is recognised and observed?

Is there anything that could have been done, either at an individual or organisational level to prevent this situation, or a similar one, from happening again?

Rosa

Rosa is 94 years old and, having become increasingly physically and mentally frail, she now lives in a nursing home. She cannot get out of her bed or chair without help and, because the staff find it difficult to make her understand what is going on around her or to encourage her to play a meaningful part in the social activities that they arrange, they tend to just ignore her unless she needs to eat or use the toilet. As Easter approached one year, the owner of the home asked the staff to organise an Easter bonnet competition as she claimed that it would cheer them all up after the winter. As very few of the residents were able to make a bonnet unaided, the staff were heavily involved in both designing and making them, to the extent that it became more of a competition between them than a meaningful event for the residents. Not wanting to exclude Rosa from the competition, she was dressed up that Easter Sunday afternoon in a hat with an Easter Bunny on it and 'to add that finishing touch', some face paint. When her relatives next visited and saw the photographs on display they were very upset. They said that, knowing Rosa as they had done for many years, it was very unlikely that she would have wanted to be part of an event such as this, and that she looked distressed on the photographs.

In what ways was Rosa's dignity compromised here?

Do you think that her family's reaction was reasonable?

How might Rosa's thoughts on the matter have been explored?

What could be done at an organisational level to help minimise the chance of this, or a similar situation, happening again?

Alvin

Alvin had been living alone and looking after himself for well over 30 years and, for the most part, his very limited vision and restricted mobility did not present any problems. He was a very active member of his community and, while it took him a long time, was happy to help others wherever he could. As he approached his 70th birthday, he decided that the time had come to move to a smaller property, as he had no use for two extra bedrooms now that his children and grandchildren had moved abroad and did not visit as often as they used to. Wondering whether he would qualify for council rented accommodation Alvin went to the housing department of his local council on a fact-finding mission. When he explained that he was considering moving house, it was suggested to him that supported housing was in short supply and that a letter from his doctor, social worker or any other advocate might help to support his case. He was rather upset about being treated this way and told his neighbour so. On hearing his account of the visit she asked why and remarked that he had done amazingly well this far to look after himself and keep a house in order too.

In what ways was Alvin's dignity compromised here?

What assumptions do you think underpinned the comments of
a) the housing department official b) the neighbour?

What could be done at an organisational level to help minimise the chance of this, or a similar situation, from happening again?

Tilly

Tilly is 30 years old and autistic. She can relax in familiar surroundings but becomes very agitated when she has to visit somewhere new, especially if the environment is noisy or crowded. On more than one occasion she has been known to lash out at some-one who has tried to welcome her and, for this reason, her carer has tended to stay at home with her as much as possible. However, Tilly needed to go to the dentist for some lengthy treatment and, fearing an outburst of 'difficult' behaviour, her carer decided to take her along to the surgery without prior explanation. When they got there, the waiting room was crowded and several small children were running around playing with bal-loons, something that Tilly had always been frightened of. As feared, she did become agitated and started flinging her arms wildly and screaming loudly, wetting herself in the process. Her carer could see that this was distressing other people, and so she manoeu-vered Tilly into a corner and restrained her until the dentist was able to carry out the treatment . Because the visit had been so traumatic, the carer took her straight home afterwards, cancelling the promised shopping trip because Tilly had not 'behaved' while they were out. While helping Tilly to change her wet clothes, she decided that inconti-nence pads were going to be necessary for any future outings.

In what ways was Tilly's dignity compromised?

How might you have acted differently?

What could be done at an organisational level to prevent this, or a similar situation, happening again?

© Jackie Martin and Sue Thompson, Working with Adults: Values into Practice www.russellhouse.co.uk

Cyril

Cyril is a white older man who has just been diagnosed with dementia. He lives on his own after his wife died, two years ago. Cyril has a daughter and son-in-law who live 50 miles away and who both work full time. Ann, Cyril's daughter, stays with him every other weekend as she wants to make sure he is 'looking after himself properly'. Cyril's neighbours have been concerned about him as he has started acting strangely and they have seen him talking to his car, which he still drives around the village. Ann has contacted social services after a neighbour has alerted her to their concerns and has requested that Cyril be 'put in a home' for his own safety.

1. What issues does this situation highlight and what dilemmas does it pose for those being called in to intervene?

2. Look at the list you made of 'what makes a good partnership' and discuss how this can be applied to working with Ann.

3. Look at the list you made of 'what makes a good partnership' and discuss how this can be applied to working with Cyril.

Cyril

It is a year later and Cyril is living in a residential home. His daughter Ann still visits him regularly. Cyril found it difficult to settle down when he first moved to his new home, as he missed his house where he had lived for 40 years. Over the past year he has become more confused and does not always recognise Ann when she visits him. Sometimes Cyril thinks Ann is his wife, Enid. Ann is concerned about Cyril, as he has become aggressive towards her and others, which is not at all like he used to be, as Cyril was a gentle, caring man.

For the following tasks, refer to your poster and try and ensure that the positive images you have captured inform the way you perform the following tasks:

• Task 1 – You are planning to have an annual review of Cyril's care. Draw up an action plan of how you are going to work with him in partnership during the review process.

• Task 2 – Ann is feeling isolated and ignored by staff at Cyril's home. She thinks they regard her as a bit of a nuisance as she rings up regularly to see how her father is. Draw up an action plan for staff to follow to work in partnership with Ann more effectively.

• Task 3 – From all the work you have done today, draw up a list of dos and don'ts for working in partnership with service users and carers.

Mavis and Bill

Part 1

Mavis was really concerned about Bill. They both lived in a residential home. Mavis had seen Bill with his son when he visited him and was uneasy about what she had witnessed. Bill's son kept asking Bill to sign cheques even though Bill told him he didn't understand what they were for and questioned the amounts of money. Bill's son had said that if he didn't sign the cheques then he wouldn't bring his grandchildren in to see him at Christmas.

Mavis had tried to talk to Bill about what she had heard, but Bill told her that it wasn't her concern and that she should keep out of his business. Mavis had seen Bill deteriorate as his dementia had advanced rapidly over the last six months and she worried that he was not remembering how often his son asked him to sign cheques.

Mavis was usually a quiet person and never troubled the staff, but she decided to talk to her keyworker about what she had heard.

Part 2

June was Mavis's keyworker. She was having a difficult time at work due to relationship difficulties with Sharon, another member of staff. June felt that she was being bullied by Sharon who is older than her and has been working in the residential home for a lot longer. June is trying to do a good job, but she knows that this is affecting her work.

Part 3

June comes into work and straightaway Mavis says she wants to talk to her. June says that she will come and speak to her in a few minutes. Two hours later June remembers that she had told Mavis that she would talk to her. June goes to find Mavis and finds her in the lounge. June starts to talk to her just as Bill's son arrives for his monthly visit. June asks what Mavis wanted to talk to her about but Mavis will not tell her and is very vague about what she wanted. June is confused but thinks that maybe Mavis is developing dementia. Mavis asks if she can talk to June later instead and June reluctantly agrees. She will come and see her after lunch.

Part 4

After lunch June goes looking for Mavis again. She sees her in the dining room but June notices that Sharon is there too. June slips away quietly so that neither Mavis nor Sharon see her.

Part 5

The next day June goes to see Mavis, as she has still not spoken to her. June finds Mavis in her bedroom getting dressed. June notices some laundry has not been collected, so she asks Mavis what she wanted while she is picking up the laundry. Mavis can't hear what she is saying, as June has her back to her. Mavis waits for June to ask her what she wants, but June goes out of the room, as she assumes that Mavis has changed her mind again.

Part 6

Mavis is getting really frustrated with June, but decides to give talking to her one last try. So, the next week when June is back on duty she asks her if she can see her after breakfast. June has an incident with Sharon where Sharon has made her look silly in front of other members of staff. When she goes to see Mavis her eyes are still red from crying. Mavis sees that June is upset and decides not to burden her with telling her about Bill. Instead, she asks how June is getting on and they have a chat about Mavis' daughters.

Mavis never does tell anyone about Bill.

1. June fails to talk to Mavis when she said she would. If she was having difficulty in finding time to talk to her, what should she have done differently?

2. June went to talk to Mavis in the lounge. What is the problem with this and what do you think she should have done?

3. June assumed that Mavis was developing dementia, as she couldn't understand her behaviour. Why do you think she assumed this and what questions do you think she should be asking herself?

4. June lets Mavis down again in the dining room. While you might understand her reasons, what effect do you think this could have on Mavis?

5. June talks to Mavis in her bedroom while Mavis is getting dressed. What should June have done differently in this situation?

6. June does eventually meet with Mavis, but Mavis gives up with the idea of telling her about Bill. What impact do you think this could have on Mavis and Bill?

Harjit

Harjit is a young man with a physical disability. He was taken into foster care when he was a small child and has now lived with his foster carers for 11 years. Harjit is now 18 years old and wants to move into his own flat. Harjit's foster carers are worried that he will not be able to cope on his own as they say he is still very young and they have always done everything for him. Harjit has a very close relationship with his carers and he wants to continue to see them on a regular basis after he has moved out of their home.

1. What do you think the problems are that need to be solved in this scenario?

2. If you were Harjit's social worker, what would be your priorities in solving these problems? Make a list of the stages you think there are in working with Harjit and his foster carers.

3. How would you make sure that Harjit's expertise on himself was valued in assessing his needs and circumstances?

4. How would you include his foster carers in the assessment?

Mitzi

Mitzi is a young woman with a learning disability. She has grown up living with her parents and brother and sister. Mitzi has always been well cared for and has had a very privileged upbringing in many ways. Her parents and her siblings have always wanted to nurture her and make sure that she hasn't had any worries of any kind. As a result of the love and concern of her family Mitzi has never had to make her own bed, do her own washing, make a meal or do any cleaning. She has spent all her time watching television or playing with video games. Although Mitzi would like to help out in the home, she believes that she is unable to and will make a mess of things. Mitzi is now 22 years old and would like to move out into her own flat as some of her friends have done.

1. What has disabled Mitzi? Is it her learning disability or the attitude and actions of her family?

2. How could Mitzi have been supported in making a contribution to the household chores?

3. What will Mitzi have to be overcome if she is to move into her own flat?

Mr Patel

Mr Patel is an older person who is living in a residential home. His wife has recently died and he is feeling completely bewildered about this loss. Mr Patel has become depressed, as he was very close to his wife and has lost interest in daily and routine activities, such as washing, shaving and changing his clothes. Mr Patel used to be a very proud man who took great care of his personal appearance.

The staff at the residential home know that Mr Patel is depressed, but are too busy to talk to him about his loss. Mr Patel has a key worker whose role it is to ensure that he receives support with his everyday activities and to let the home manager know if there are any concerns about Mr Patel.

Mr Patel's keyworker is a new member of staff who hasn't received a proper induction due to staff shortages and who has never worked with older people before. The keyworker knows that Mr Patel is not washing, shaving or changing his clothes, but thinks he must always have been a person who didn't really look after himself, so doesn't mention this to anyone or talk to Mr Patel about it.

Mr Patel stops eating and starts to stay in bed all day. Staff ask him if he wants to get up and offer him cups of tea, but he refuses. His keyworker is worried about him but does not know what to do about her concerns. There have been frequent changes of staff in the residential home resulting in no one, apart from the keyworker, being aware that Mr Patel has been in bed for weeks.

The keyworker finally decides to talk to the manager of the home who goes to see Mr Patel. The manager calls Mr Patel's GP, who visits. The GP is shocked to see how thin Mr Patel is, as he had seen him six months previously. The GP discovers that Mr Patel has pressure sores which are fairly deep.

1. What has made Mr Patel 'vulnerable'?

2. What should have been done differently in the residential home?

3. How could Mr Patel have been supported in a way which didn't make him vulnerable?

Ernest

Ernest tells a member of staff that he wants to talk to them. The member of staff asks Ernest where he wants to talk to them and he indicates the lounge as no one else is in there. When they sit down to talk it is obvious that Ernest is very nervous and he shuffles in his chair quite a lot. When Ernest does talk he tells the member of staff that he thinks that a resident is being physically abused by another member of staff. He says that he has heard the other resident crying in the night after the particular member of staff goes into their bedroom. Ernest also says that he has noticed bruises on the resident's wrists which he thinks look like he has been gripped or held down forcibly.

Victor

Victor is a support worker in a residential home called 'The Elms' for young adults with a physical impairment. Victor has not worked in social care before as he was made redundant from a job in a factory. He was looking forward to working in a different environment but was nervous, as he didn't know what was expected of him or what the staff group would be like.

When Victor started working he was surprised by how friendly the staff were with each other. Victor really liked this, but noticed that staff often ignored the service users and had conversations when they were with them that did not include them.

Victor also noticed that staff did not eat with the people they supported but kept special treats aside for themselves and ate separately. When Victor asked about this practice he was told that it was one of the perks of working there - nice free food and a chance to socialise with other staff members away from the residents.

Victor often heard staff telling stories about the service users which made fun of them. Victor didn't really think this was appropriate but laughed at the stories as he liked the other members of staff and didn't want to offend them. Victor thought it was probably all right to do this, as these stories were never recounted to managers or to any other service users.

Victor was looking forward to going away on holiday with the residents as he had heard stories about how enjoyable this had been last year. Victor went to the meeting in the spring where holidays were discussed. He had heard the staff discussing their holiday preferences before the meeting and noticed that it was only these preferences which were put forward as options for possible destinations.

After the meeting Victor heard two versions of what had happened. The first version was the account relayed to managers where it was said that it was the choice of the residents where they went. The second account was the more private account between members of staff where they were looking forward to going away on their choice of holidays. There was also discussion about how staff could have time away from residents to do what they really wanted to do.

1. What is helpful about the workplace culture of The Elms? Who is it helpful for?

2. What is unhelpful about the workplace culture of The Elms? Who is it unhelpful for?

3. What do you think should be done differently at the Elms? Would this improve the workplace culture?

Electronic supply of the worksheets and case studies from *Working with Adults*

If you would like to receive a PDF of the worksheets and case studies from this manual, please complete the form below, tear out this page, and return it to us. Please note that photocopies are not acceptable, nor are applications made through e-mail, phone or fax.

Please keep a copy of the completed form for your own records.

This PDF is free.

Please note

RHP reserves the right to withdraw this offer at any time without any prior notice.

RHP reserves the right to qualify or reject any application which it is not completely satisfied is on an original torn-out page from the back of a purchased manual.

Terms and conditions for use of the worksheets and case studies from *Working with Adults*

1. Buying a copy of *Working with Adults* and completing this form gives the individual who signs the form permission to use the materials in the PDF that will be sent from RHP for their own use only.

2. The hard copies that they then print from the PDF are subject to the same permissions and restrictions that are set out in the 'photocopying permission' section at the front of this manual.

3. Under no circumstances should they forward or copy the electronic materials to anyone else.

4. If the person who signs this form wants a licence to be granted for wider use of the electronic materials within their organisation, network or client base, they must make a request directly to RHP fully detailing the proposed use. All requests will be reviewed on their own merits.

> • If the request is made when submitting this form to RHP, the request should be made in writing and should accompany this form.

> • If the request is made later, it should be made in an email sent to help@russelhouse.co.uk, and should not only fully detail the proposed use, but also give the details of the person whose name and contact details were on the original application form.

RHP and the authors expect this honour system to be followed respectfully, by individuals and organisations whom we in turn respect. RHP will act to protect authors' copyright if they become aware of it being infringed.

I would like to receive a free PDF of the worksheets and case studies from *Working with Adults*

*Name _____

 *Address _____

 _____

 _____

 _____

*Post code _____

*Contact phone number _____

*e-mail address _____ (to which the PDF will be e-mailed)

I have read, and accept, the terms and conditions on the reverse of this page. I understand that RHP may use this information to contact me about other matters and publications, but that RHP will not make my details available to any other organisations.

*Signed _____ *Date _____

* All sections marked with an asterisk **must be completed**, or the form will be returned to the postal address given here.

Please return to:
Russell House Publishing
4 St George's House
Uplyme Rd
Lyme Regis
Dorset
DT7 3LS

Learning for Practice

This manual is the second in a series of learning and development resources to be published by Russell House Publishing under the guidance of series editor, Neil Thompson. Each manual will offer invaluable support and guidance for training and development staff in organisations; lecturers and tutors in colleges and universities; and managers keen to play an active role in promoting learning within their team or staff group.

Already published:

• **Meaning and Values**   By Bernard Moss and Neil Thompson

Drawing on three books in the *Theory into Practice* series (*Values* and *Religion and Spirituality* by Bernard Moss and *Power and Empowerment* by Neil Thompson) this learning resource manual offers important guidance for people delivering training and development for staff across the helping professions who are committed to promoting best practice.

Other titles confirmed for publication include:

• **Tackling bullying and harassment in the workplace** By Neil Thompson

Sadly, bullying and harassment are far more prevalent in organisations than most people realise. This learning resource will be an excellent guide for anyone involved in delivering training and development for staff and managers across the whole range of 'people professions'.

• **Introducing solution-focused brief therapy**   By Steve Myers and Judith Milner

Building on the Theory into Practice book, Solution-focused approaches by Steve Myers, this well-crafted resource will provide a firm foundation for delivering high-quality learning opportunities for students, staff and managers. Adopting solution-focused approaches offers excellent potential for effective practice, and this manual provides important guidance on how to help people build up their knowledge and skills.

• **Promoting equality, valuing diversity**   By Neil Thompson

Neil Thompson's work on anti-discriminatory practice has become very highly respected for its clarity, successfully combining theoretical depth with practical usefulness. Building on his success in this area, this manual will provide a range of exercises carefully designed to enable participants to maximise their learning about these complex and challenging issues.

Further manuals are planned for the series.

Details will be available at www.russellhouse.co.uk when ready.

Titles in the *Theory into Practice* series
Series editor: Neil Thompson

Solution-focused approaches   By Steve Myers

Helpful, empowering and hopeful... this introductory book can help anyone who wants to learn more about how to embed these qualities in their work. It explores the theoretical assumptions that underpin solution-focused brief therapy, assumptions about people and what is helpful in promoting change through empowering them to take appropriate responsibility for their lives. It addresses ☐ how to develop solution-focused practice in a reflectice way ☐ principles and techniques involved in the work ☐ how it can inform anti-oppressive practice. 120 pages 978-1-905541-18-8. 2007

Safeguarding adults   By Jackie Martin

For anyone who works with adults who are in need of care or support and who are unable to protect themselves from harm, exploitation or loss of independence. This book shows the need to offer them respect as citizens alongside protection from abuse. It addresses: how anyone can create and perpetuate the experience of being 'vulnerable'; how we can address this as a matter of personal responsibility and in workplace cultures and practices; what we can do if someone is being subjected to abuse; why we some-times don't challenge other workers; why we should; and what happens when we do. "Case illustrations are used to good effect... The emphasis on antidiscriminatory practice is excellent." Community Care. 112 pages. 978-1-903855-98-0. 2007

Values   By Bernard Moss

Exploring the value base of people work involves travelling in areas that may seem familiar. But values can be eroded by pressure and anxiety. So new insights can reinforce integrity and re-energise commitment. "Knowing ourselves is a prerequisite for reflective practice." Community Care. This is "a brief, user friendly exploration of the impact that our values bring to our work. The author really does 'know his stuff' and is passionate to share it." Addiction Today. 128 pages. 978-1-903855-89-8. 2007

Age discrimination .   By Sue Thompson

"Deals with the subject of age discrimination in a no-nonsense way...highly recommended... both informative and challenging." Rostrum. "Interspersed with personal and practice-focused exercises that fuel further thought." Community Care. "Extremely accessible... It draws from an extensive literature base, is well-structured ... an important addition to all bookshelves." Nursing Standard. "A timely textbook... well researched... a useful resource... recommended." Ethics & Social Welfare. 104 pages. 978-1-903855-59-1. 2005

Religion and spirituality   By Bernard Moss

"Intended to help staff engage with people's religion and spirituality, if appropriate... It guides the reader through ways of celebrating diversity, fostering resilience and chall-enging discrimination." Care & Health. "A cogent, compelling and clear exposition of the theory and practice of religion and spirituality in human services... particularly welcome, as it comes from a respected social work educator of great integrity." Health and Social Care in the Community. "Indispensable for holistic service provision... displays an impressive degree of cultural sensitivity toward people of faith... An extremely useful resource." Journal of Social Work. 120 pages. 978-1-903855-57-7. 2005